Furnace Murder

True Story of the

Horrific Murder of Mrs. Cody

Harvey W. Rowe

and

David K. Dodd

David K. Dodd

BAY CREEK PUBLISHING

FURNACE MURDER
July 2014

Cover design by Patrick Fisher.

Library of Congress Control Number 2014943468

ISBN 978-0-9835670-3-5

Published by
Bay Creek Publishing
PO Box 546
Fish Creek, WI 54212
BayCreekPublishing.com

In Memory of

Harvey Rowe (1934-2004)

Schema of Neighborhood of Fifth Avenue, Sturgeon Bay, in 1948

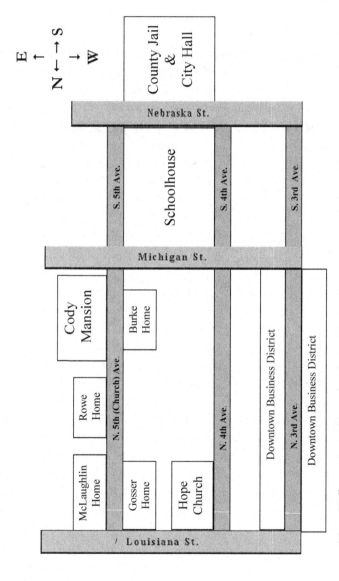

Note. Kellstrom's service station is one block north (left) of Hope Church. Mrs. Cody's two rental properties are approximately 0.8 mi. from the mansion, one to the north (where William Drews lived) and one to the south. The Greystone Castle is located near the south property. (Map is not to scale.)

Contents

Preface

Harvey Rowe and I have coauthored *Furnace Murder*, but we never met! In 2013, one of Harvey's many friends contacted me and told me all about him and his manuscript. Like all of his friends, this one was saddened by the fact that Harvey had died in 2004 before his work could be published. As a local author perhaps I could help, the friend hoped.

That was my introduction to Harvey and his manuscript. As I read it, I was struck by several things. The content was fascinating and the writing skillful. It was clear I had my work cut out for me, because at 282 typewritten pages the manuscript was far too lengthy. After devoting at least a dozen years to its writing, Harvey had simply tried to include too much. He wanted to document every detail of the life of the famous neighbor of whom he was so fond. He also wanted the book to be a glowing tribute to Sheriff Hallie Rowe, his father and hero, and, in fact, originally titled the manuscript *About My Father's Business*. Finally, of course, there was the small-town murder that made national headlines.

As I worked to turn Harvey's expansive manuscript into a publishable book, my primary consideration was attracting a variety of readers. I knew that history buffs would be pleased with the details about past life in Sturgeon Bay, Wisconsin, and local readers would enjoy hearing about Sheriff Rowe and his crime-fighting counterparts. And what reader would not be fascinated by the exploits of a feisty adolescent—Harvey—who lived in the sheriff's quarters in the county jail! In the end, though, I knew it would be the heinous "furnace murder" that would most captivate readers, just as it did the townspeople of Sturgeon Bay in 1948.

A few words about accuracy, authorship, and word usage. *Furnace Murder* is a true story based upon generally accepted knowledge, newspaper articles, court records, statements and memories of many participants and, of course, the recollections of Harvey Rowe. The murder itself is detailed in Chapter 11. Immediately prior to the killing, a man and his victim had a brief but crucial conversation. Afterwards, he roamed the crime scene for about twenty-five minutes. My description of their words and thoughts is speculative, but it is derived in part from the killer's confession, forensic evidence, and facts generally known about the murderer and victim.

The book is divided into four parts. The first three reflect Harvey's original manuscript, including an epilogue. Although I edited heavily for length, combined chapters, and modified some chapter titles, I tried to stay true to the original while improving readability. The personal pronoun "I" refers to Harvey, as he tells the story from his own viewpoint.

I solely have authored the Prologue and Part IV, which includes two additional chapters and the Afterword. My goal was to address several remaining mysteries: What was the character of the killer, and to what did he actually confess? What were his motives—was the furnace murder spontaneous, or premeditated? And was this the first time he had taken a life?

In the end, there is the mystery of Harvey Rowe himself. As a fourteen-year-old in 1948, he had a front-row seat as the harrowing events of the murder unfolded. Surely he was deeply affected. To what extent was he able to move on? Did the manuscript that he spent so many years developing actually contribute to his own demise?

Readers will be challenged by all of these questions—there are no easy answers!

David K. Dodd

Part I

Prologue

He walked up the sidewalk to her porch, climbed the five steps, and knocked at her door. She answered and invited him in. He asked her for a favor but she declined. He repeated his request and again she turned him down. With his right fist, he struck her in the side of the head and she crumpled. Standing over her, he wasn't sure what to do. He gathered her in his arms, gently, and headed for the stairs leading to the cellar. She moaned softly.

The stairway was narrow and he had to angle his way down, taking each step carefully. His hand scraped the rough block wall and he cried out in pain. He took the final four steps quickly and found himself standing in the middle of the cellar, still holding the body. What to do with it? He spotted the furnace.

A moment later he bent down a little, swung open the door to the firepot, and readied himself to stuff her in, headfirst. Her limp body moved ever so slightly—was it his trembling arms or was she still alive?

He recommitted himself to the only choice he had and began to feed her body in, as though it were a log. It took some maneuvering, because the firepot was small. At last, he folded her spindly legs in and closed door. He heard a muffled hiss—could it be from *her?* Probably just the fire, he hoped.

It was all over. He stood briefly in front of the furnace, his arms straight at his sides, his head bowed slightly. What had he done? He forced himself to consider his next move. Before ascending the cellar steps, he reached for the dial on the furnace and turned up the heat.

At the town's school building a block away, children and adolescents sat in their classrooms, studying the clock in anticipation of lunch recess. They began to notice an odd smell and looked around, catching each other's eyes. At lunch, they made wild, crude guesses about the source of the foul odor. By the time they walked home after school, some held their noses as the horrible stench permeated the entire neighborhood.

1

The Lady Next Door

I had a terrific childhood that, in my eyes, began the summer I was eight. My family had just moved into a new house in the best part of town in the best little city in the world, Sturgeon Bay, Wisconsin. I had never seen Dad happier than he was that day, and I was right there with him. Mom was tickled too.

Six years later my childhood ended just as suddenly as it started. My friend was murdered in the most gruesome manner, and I would never again look at life in quite the same way.

~ ~ ~

One of my fondest early memories was Sunday mornings when Mom and I would walk across the old bridge linking the east and west sides of town to St. Peter's Lutheran Church. I didn't even mind walking a mile, because it was our routine and I always liked church.

I don't remember Dad ever making the walk with us. He was the State Conservation Warden—"game warden"—and had been since long before I arrived in 1934. Many of my earliest memories were of Dad's job. For example, he told Mom he couldn't go to church because game poachers would catch on about his Sunday morning routine and take free reign. Still, he sometimes slept in. Any other day of the week, Dad was up and about by 5:30. I could never understand why anyone would get up that early unless there was a gun pointing at his head. But Dad explained that dawn was prime time for game, and thus for poachers.

Furnace Murder

Dad never took me to work with him back then, but I could always imagine him armed with binoculars and a handgun, searching the woods for law violators. A rumor even circulated around the county that Hallie Rowe was "part Indian"—the only explanation for his uncanny ability to sneak around undetected. To me, Dad was everywhere, kind of like God.

My parents came to Sturgeon Bay in 1928, when Dad became warden. As newlyweds they stayed in a single room of a private residence a block from downtown. They really liked their live-in landlord, who was especially helpful in getting them acquainted with the community. But to save on heating costs, Mrs. Washburn kept their room so cold in the winter that they could hardly stand it. Eventually my parents traded their fondness for the landlady for a bigger place with a thermostat of their own!

We moved into our brand new, brick home at 22 North Church Street on July 22, 1942. I'll never forget our house number because it was etched into the brick above our front door. Years later, the city changed all the street names—Church became Fifth Avenue—and every house in town got a new street number except ours. By then Dad was sheriff, and no one had the nerve to tell him that he'd have to chisel out that brick above the threshold.

Game warden was a very respectable job but it didn't pay much, so my parents had to save for years to afford their dream home. I remember Dad was a heavy smoker, but he gave it up entirely so he could afford the fireplace he wanted so much. He was so proud of his new house that, during its construction, he'd swing by on a daily basis to oversee the progress being made by the carpenters, electricians, plumbers, and masons. Perfectionist that he was, he probably drove the workers to complete distraction. But he wanted everything just right, and he assured my mother that the new house would be so nice that she wouldn't have to work so hard.

He was right about the house but wrong about Mom's work. She was so meticulous about everything that she seemed to work all day, every day. People would ask Dad how his wife liked the new home, and he would reply, "She's still after the dirt." He meant that Mom couldn't be satisfied until every bit of soil was ridded from our clothes and every nook of our house, but of course it never was.

Dad bought the lot from Alice (Allie) McLaughlin, who lived just north of us in the house on the corner. On the other side of us was a mansion, the most famous house in town. It needed repairs and the old wooden fence that surrounded it was falling down, but even a kid like me could tell that long ago it had really been *something*.

Dad had Allie watch for trespassers while our house was under construction. It was a good plan but the very first trespassers she caught were me and a friend—I just couldn't resist a close look at the place I'd soon call home. I tried to explain to Mrs. McLaughlin that I *owned* the house—at least my dad did—but she said she didn't care and kicked me out anyway. Later, Dad took me next door to introduce me to Allie, and after that she never ordered me away again. In fact she was pretty friendly.

So life in 1942 sure looked great. I never even thought about World War II that much, though the adults were always talking about it. Dad was game warden and I was his son. We had just settled into a brand new house in a good location with great neighbors. Downtown was only two blocks away and the big schoolhouse where I would attend third grade was only a half-block from home!

~ ~ ~

Everyone in Sturgeon Bay seemed to know Mrs. R.P. Cody. They knew she lived—and had forever—in the grand old Victorian mansion in the center of town. And they knew she was filthy rich, or once had been. In reality, though, no one knew her at all. That's what I concluded after she and I became friends.

The three-story, fifteen-room mansion was famous. It had been built at the turn of the century, but despite showing its age it was still quite a showplace. Dark green in color with tasteful cream-colored borders, it rested on a large tract of land that extended nearly a block from Fifth to Sixth Avenue. The wrap-around front porch was huge, and it had several dramatic wooden pillars supporting the roof.

Furnace Murder

Perhaps most striking was the enormous column that rose from the porch clear past the third-floor roof—it made the mansion seem like a fortress.

The mansion held a certain mystique because Mrs. Cody, now in her eighties, lived there alone and had become isolated from the outside world. Once a prominent citizen, she now ventured out only to shop, attend occasional meetings of the Woman's Club, or walk to Sunday services at Hope Congregational Church a block-and-a-half away.

Generations of children had passed the mansion on their way to school, either to the city school a block south or to the Catholic grade school a block north. The wooden fence that surrounded the mansion had deteriorated badly over the years and its paint was now almost entirely stripped away by the harsh Wisconsin winters. Halloween attracted vandals to the mansion like flies to honey, and Mrs. Cody had little choice but to hire someone to guard the fence and keep trouble-makers away.

The interior of her house, seldom seen now by anyone but her closest friends, was truly awesome. Hand-carved wooden panels adorned the walls and inlaid shelves were tastefully filled with bric-a-brac. Although I never saw the second or third floors, I was tempted by the huge winding stairwell that led upstairs. The downstairs rooms still exuded the same magnificence that they had at the turn of the century. Little old Mrs. Cody tried her best to maintain the gigantic mansion inside and out. She did pretty well in the housekeeping department but was lousy at repairs.

She told me that as a young girl, her family had very little—her father labored hard as a gardener but could never get ahead. Mrs. Cody knew the value of hard work, and even as an old lady she remained energetic and nimble. Amazed by her resolve, I often watched as she climbed a ladder with a pail of water to wash windows or walls.

In earlier years she had employed helpers and live-in servants, but later she became so frugal she tried to go it alone. Was her thrift truly necessary or a product of an unrealistic fear of going broke? That was a question local residents debated for years.

Rowe and Dodd

In the cold months Mrs. Cody began closing off part of her spacious second floor and the entire third floor and lived solely on the main floor. There she slept on a tiny daybed right next to bookcases that still contained her husband's old law books. Over the years she abandoned even the second floor. Each morning she would dutifully make her little bed and prepare a sparse breakfast. For every meal she meticulously arranged the dining room table, complete with a silverware setting for one. Afterwards she washed everything and neatly stacked it away in the cupboard.

It was the outside of the mansion, and its large surrounding grounds, that really got her down. Behind the mansion were two dilapidated sheds, one of which served as a garage for her old car from years before, when she still drove. From time to time, the condition of the grounds bothered her so much she would break down and hire someone to do the necessary work.

One of her hired hands was my uncle Herb Rowe, who came to visit us almost every summer. He paid Mrs. Cody a few dollars to park his car in her garage. One year she hired him to paint her entire house, a big job that took most of the summer. When the task was finally done and it was time to get paid, Herb was nervous that she was going to refund his parking fee and just declare everything "even up." But she was real fair and paid what he asked.

Mrs. Cody no longer had city water and hadn't for years! To save a few dollars a month, she discontinued municipal service and relied on her large cistern for water, which was good for washing and cleaning but was undrinkable. That meant she had to make daily trips to the public schoolhouse for free city water. After filling her galvanized pail, she made the trek back home, transferring the heavy load from one hand to another every few steps. Watching her fascinated me! It wasn't until years later that I realized I should have offered to help. People ridiculed her for relying on free water and other similar habits, but she ignored them, or at least pretended to.

Throughout the years Mrs. Cody retreated further and further into a world of her own, surrounded only by memories of the happy years. In later years few people had the opportunity to know her well. But her few close friends knew she was kind and delightful in her own way.

Furnace Murder

~ ~ ~

The day we moved into our new house, Dad saw Mrs. Cody standing on her front lawn and took me over to meet her. He was especially concerned that I treat our elderly neighbor with kindness and respect. All it took was that initial encounter for Mrs. Cody and me to became like old friends. She liked my parents too. Dad assured her, "If you ever need any help, just let me know." It must have comforted her to have a law enforcement officer living next door, especially since Dad's official car was always parked out front, with its red light and siren mounted prominently on the hood.

Many people laughed about Mrs. Cody's penny-pinching ways, how she shopped at local stores asking for "a nickel's worth of this" or "a dime's worth of that." Local merchants chattered about her shopping exploits and tried to one-up each other with a new story about her cheapness. For example, I remember hearing that Mrs. Cody was taunted by the owner of the downtown meat market where she shopped for just enough meat for her evening meal. The testy merchant reportedly waved a small hamburger patty under her nose and jeered, "That's all you get for five cents. Fresh enough for you?" Even now, as I look back, I still take Mrs. Cody's side on that one. No one had modern refrigeration back then, so she couldn't have kept large amounts of meat without it spoiling. Besides, she ate like a bird.

Not everyone ridiculed Mrs. Cody, though. Some respected not only her frugality but her kindness, especially toward children. One child from the neighborhood still remembers that Mrs. Cody and a friend would make summer trips to Michigan to pick blueberries. Mrs. Cody would also harvest fragile vines that bore orange berries, and back home she'd dry the vines and tie them together to form little bouquets. Then she invited local children to sell them around town for five cents each, earning them a penny or two for each bouquet they sold—a lot of money for little children at the time. And she would always send a small bag of blueberries for the kids to snack on.

Despite the fact that she owned a lot of property, Mrs. Cody had very little actual income. There was no Social Security in those days and no retirement benefits—her only cash flow was the mere pittance she took in from the renters in the two run-down houses she owned. With property taxes to pay, plus repairs, it was no wonder she was frugal.

Still, many people around town gloated because Mrs. Cody, once so wealthy and prominent, had been reduced to miserliness. Hard-hearted adults spread awful rumors, which often focused on her second and third marriages and included wild speculation about marital affairs and blackmail. The most outrageous one I ever heard was that Mrs. Cody literally starved her daughter to death.

Even some librarians could be small-minded. Mrs. Cody once objected to the policy that many books could only be rented rather than checked out for free. To skirt the policy, she would sometimes read rental books while seated comfortably in the library. That led two unrelenting librarians to concoct a new rule that patrons could read rental books only while standing. They knew the elderly Mrs. Cody could only read a page or two under such rules and would be forced to either rent the books or leave.

Many of the kids in town quickly picked up on the meanness of their elders. Some said her old house was haunted and that Mrs. Cody was a witch. Often they stole grapes that grew on vines covering the old fence, and when she attempted to chase them away, they would taunt her or even pelt her with the fruit.

They put pins in her doorbell to prevent it from functioning and broke loose slats from the deteriorating fence any time they felt like it. It about broke my heart to see Mrs. Cody with hammer and nails, kneeling next to the fence, attempting to repair it. The very worst thing I ever heard kids say was that old lady Cody killed all three of her husbands and stashed their bodies away in the cellar.

One cold, blustery night during our first winter on Church Street, Mrs. Cody appeared in our front yard, holding a package. She climbed the six steps to the front door and rang the bell. Before we could answer, though, a harsh gust of wind swung the storm door wide open, knocking her down onto the concrete porch and halfway down the stairs. The poor little lady weighed barely ninety pounds, no match for such a wind. When we answered the door, she was righting herself and had a smile on her face, along with good intentions in her heart. More importantly, she had a Christmas gift for me!

After we got her in the house and made sure she was all right, we gave her something warm to drink. I wanted to open my present right away, but Mom and Dad made me put it under the tree and wait for Christmas Day. It turned out to be a card game called "Flinch." I knew Mrs. Cody loved playing cards and used to host a ton of card parties at the mansion. Perhaps I realized at the time how special that gift was— or maybe I just couldn't get Mom and Dad to play it with me. Either way, I never opened it and have kept it in mint condition ever since.

Mrs. Cody's front lawn was adorned with a couple of old crab-apple trees, and every year she told us to take what we wanted. Mom always said they weren't much good—even I agreed, though I'd eat almost anything. But we always picked a few apples so her feelings wouldn't be hurt. Mom was a terrific baker, and to reciprocate she would always bake something special for her, *without* the crabapples. It was my job to take it next door, and usually I'd get invited in and get to sample Mom's pie or her famous Parker House rolls, even if supper time was right around the corner.

She was really a likable old lady and an interesting person too, and I'm not saying it just because she gave me presents and candy. She could spin good stories and always kept up on current events. It disturbed her that the old town clock at the bank had been removed. Many times she told me, "We should have a town clock so that people know what time it is!" There might have been some self-interest involved, because she herself never wore a watch.

Whenever I went to the mansion, Mom always made me call beforehand to warn Mrs. Cody that I was on my way. She was particular about wanting to be called in advance, she didn't like surprise visitors. I loved taking treats to her—she was always so pleased by our favors. When I got back home, Mom always made me repeat exactly what she had said. Thinking back, I'm sure it made Mom happy to do something special for the little old lady who always ate alone. Why we never invited her over to our house for dinner is a real mystery.

Rowe and Dodd

Almost always, whenever I showed up at her front door, she asked me in: "Can't you just stay for a few minutes to talk with me? Come in and visit." Unless I was really busy, in I went. We'd take our places in the sitting room and chat about current happenings around town or in the neighborhood. She let me do most of the talking.

On the wall was a picture of Wild Bill Cody with a hatchet hanging underneath it. When I asked her about it, she told me that Wild Bill was her cousin by marriage, several times removed. I wasn't sure what that last part meant but was sure impressed she was related to one of my heroes. I could tell she was real proud of that picture and pleased I was interested.

Rarely did she talk about her former life as a turn-of-the-century society matron. Probably the memories were too painful for her, or she thought I wouldn't appreciate it all. One time she told me about attending the opening day of the World's Fair in Chicago. In 1893! I could tell it was a treasured memory, one of the highlights of her life. She also shared that her mother was from a small town in New York named Canandaigua. Before I left, she made me pronounce it correctly three times—what a mouthful!

I think back to all the horrible rumors that Mrs. Cody suffered in silence. She must have known that trying to refute idiots would only make things worse, so she seemed to retreat further into the nearly make-believe world of her past—when she, like the mansion, stood tall with the full respect of the community. At the end she became distrustful of almost everyone except her closest friends. She lost her appetite and continued to lose more and more weight. She even suspected that someone might be sending her poisoned candy, perhaps to kill her and take over the estate.

Once she brought us a beautiful box of candy, which we suspected had been a gift from someone. The next day she was at the door again, asking for the candy back and replacing it with another gift. "You didn't eat any, did you?" she wanted to know. As it turned out, she was afraid she had poisoned *us* with it! I could tell how relieved she was to retrieve the box of candy, unopened.

Furnace Murder

Another time when I was at the mansion, I was snooping around a little and opened one of her dining room cabinets. I was amazed to see a number of boxes of candy, neatly stacked one upon another. Mrs. Cody was too fearful to eat the candy yet too frugal to throw it away.

~ ~ ~

Looking back I have so many great memories of Mrs. Cody, but I also have some distressing flashbacks. In one recurring dream, I see her alone in that old mansion at night in the dead of winter, trees leafless, the wind howling. A dim light silohuettes her as she sits quietly in her rocker, covered by a thin lap blanket. The front yard, surrounded by a dilapidated fence six feet high, has become a spooky cemetery. There are no graves, just headstones nailed by heavy spikes to bare trees. Like sap, blood oozes from the bark.

It is an image that still haunts me. I have to force it from my mind and remind myself that I always tried to be kind to her. We were good friends.

2

From Zero to Zooey

Dad was always bragging how "centrally located" our new house was, how *convenient* it was to everything. It's true, we were within walking distance of anything we needed—two blocks from the downtown business district, a block from the post office, and within view of my school. The county jail was also just two blocks away, right next to the courthouse. Add in City Hall, the fire and police departments, the library, where I spent many hours, and the museum, which I also frequented, and it was true—we lived at the epicenter of the world.

Several churches were located on or near our street, thus its name "Church Street." These included Christ the King Episcopal next to the Cody mansion; Hope Congregational, where Mrs. Cody attended; the Methodist Church; and the biggest church in the county, St. Joseph's Catholic Church.

Our neighborhood had it all, including a large, vicious dog named "Zero." I liked both the animal and its owner, Allie McLaughlin. Except for Mrs. Cody, Allie was my favorite neighbor. She was getting along in years but was not deteriorating nearly as rapidly as her house, next door to ours. Allie and her husband Dick tried to keep things up but they were overmatched. The house was falling apart—it hadn't been painted for years, plus the garage was one strong wind away from collapse. But Allie had more important things to do.

She was in several civic organizations, including the Eastern Star, and she frequently attended gala functions at the Masonic Temple. How I remember her exiting the back door of her house, wearing a long formal dress adorned with a corsage! Dick would hold up her flowing attire so that it wouldn't drag through their dusty, unpaved driveway. Into the garage she disappeared and out she came with a roar, behind the wheel of their ancient car. Off to the gala, a sight to behold!

Back to ground Zero. That dog guarded the McLaughlin house all right, but the *yard* was his absolute domain. Plenty of traffic passed their corner lot at Church and Louisiana. The cars were safe but pedestrians feared for their lives! Typically Zero lay in the yard, like a giant, sleeping crocodile, and anyone could see he was tethered by a heavy chain. But looks were deceiving.

Like most creatures, Zero had his favorites who he'd let pass with hardly the raising of an eyebrow. His enemies, though, could expect a full-fledged charge with one of two outcomes: Either Zero would reach the end of his chain and be violently whiplashed, or the victim would feel the dog's wrath on the calf or thigh. I spent a lot of time in the summer watching the action from our front porch.

Zero took a particular aversion to a neighbor I'll call Zooey. She was not a pleasant person and most humans shared the dog's dislike of her. Through experience Zooey knew exactly how far Zero could range on his leash, and she enjoyed tempting him by walking just beyond his reach. One day I watched her approach his corner. She was wearing a fancy hat and a bright red coat—that lady sure knew how to dress! But she was a matador with a bright red cape, provoking a wild bull. In half a second Zero reached full speed. This time, instead of whiplash, the dog's chain broke and he was all over Zooey.

Allie must have been watching from her window too, because she was on the scene in two seconds, grabbing the broken chain and tugging the giant dog off his victim. Allie knew it was Zero who was technically in the wrong, so she gave him a swift kick, more for show than punishment. Fortunately Zooey wasn't hurt but her coat was badly torn, and she was plenty hot about it. A good seamstress, Allie promised to repair the coat, and a day or two later she returned it to Zooey in perfect condition. There was never a lawsuit, never an attorney or police involved.

I was one of Zero's closest friends. I always brought him scraps from the dinner table, especially nice juicy bones that he'd enjoy for hours. He was not so keen on Mom, though. She had permission to hang our freshly washed clothes on Allie's nice clothesline out back. It was perfectly fine with Allie but unacceptable to Zero. One day I saw Mom come dashing home, her basket of fresh clothes left behind, Zero at her heels. This time I had to root for the human. Allie returned later with our clothes but no apology—it was entirely the *dog's* fault, not hers, and everyone agreed.

I spent a lot of time with Zero. Every day he would wait for me to come home from school, and the two of us did all kinds of tricks like rolling over and shaking hands. One afternoon Zero was nowhere to be found, so I headed for Allie's door to demand what she had done with my playmate. On the porch was a large pile of rugs, and like any kid I stepped *on* the rugs rather than going around. I lost my balance and fell. Before getting back up, I peeked under the pile and spotted my friend—Zero was dead!

I couldn't believe it and ran home, crying. Mom explained that Allie could no longer take care of the dog and had put him down— make that *out*, with the rugs. I screamed, *Why, Mom? Why didn't she give Zero to me?* Mom didn't have a good answer, and though I thought a thousand times about asking Allie my question, I never did. Now that I think of it, another question I should have asked her was why she left Zero out on the porch under a pile of rugs.

The other neighbor lady I remember vividly was Loretta Burke, who lived directly across the street from the Cody mansion. She was not nearly as fond of kids as either Mrs. Cody or Allie but was a good neighbor, and I considered her a friend. There were a few other kids on our block besides me, but Sadie, Allie, and Loretta were my best neighborhood friends. I never had the nerve to admit that to the kids at school, though.

I got off on the wrong foot with Mrs. Burke shortly after my family moved to our new house. Some school friends and I were going through her garbage can, and she took real exception to it, yelling out at us. Later it got back to my mom that Mrs. Burke told another neighbor I was a "real corker." Because I was only eight, I wasn't sure what that meant, but I took it as a compliment.

Furnace Murder

Over the years, Loretta and Sadie had become close friends and visited each other nearly every day. Sometimes Mrs. Cody would even stop at the Burkes for coffee and rolls. I couldn't help but feel a little hurt that Loretta never invited *me* over.

Mrs. Burke passed the evenings by sitting on her enclosed front porch, watching the neighborhood action. She was a heavy smoker, and I was clever enough to detect when she was out there in the dark because of the glow of her cigarette. I doubt she could see me, because I always turned off the lights to reduce window glare. Plus I didn't smoke back then. As I think back, it's funny to think of the two of us on opposite sides of Church Street, staring into the dark night, waiting for something to happen.

Mrs. Burke had a distinct advantage over me. Living directly across the street from the mansion, she could keep closer tabs on all the activities of little old Mrs. Cody, as well as anyone who came to Sadie's front door. I could barely see the front porch from our place. With hawk-like eyes, Loretta knew Mrs. Cody's habits like her own. I often wonder if Sadie knew that she had her very own detective living across the street!

~ ~ ~

In the spring of 1944, Mom took sick. She hadn't been feeling well for some time and before we could blink, she was scheduled for surgery. I was only nine and didn't fully comprehend how sick she was, but years later Mom told me that some of her friends, afraid she might die, paid her a special visit at the hospital.

What a lousy coincidence that the state Conservation Department chose this critical time in our lives to transfer Dad from Door County all the way to West Bend, near Milwaukee. He had only three days to set his house in order. Dad was convinced that the order was motivated by spite. A former state assemblyman who was cozy with the Department still carried a grudge from years before. As game warden, Dad had enforced the gaming laws so well that the man's friends couldn't go "deer shining" and bag deer out of season—so now the man was targeting my dad. Under civil service rules Dad couldn't be

Rowe and Dodd

fired without cause, but the Department could make life so miserable you quit. That's what this "administrative transfer" was all about, according to Dad.

Once before, in 1937, the Department attempted to transfer Dad. That time, however, conservation groups in the county mounted a strong campaign, complete with petition drives, to keep him as warden. The *Door County Advocate* even jumped into the fray, stating: "The fact that he has a record that is endorsed by the people of this county should be sufficient argument that Warden Hallie Rowe should continue his work in Door County."

Dad won that battle but the current one was a different story. Troubles beset—a dying wife, a little boy to manage, and a new home that still required work. His enemies had the upper hand, and three days later Dad threw in the towel and resigned. He lost not only the job he'd held for sixteen years but also his state pension.

We were in deep trouble, but fate intervened and our lives took a new twist. Mom improved and returned home from the hospital. The Sturgeon Bay Police Department decided that it needed an extra officer, and Dad was hired to work evenings and nights. The Rowes were making a quick comeback.

Sheriff Harry Brann's term was expiring, and the state constitution prohibited him from seeking an additional term. Several of Dad's supporters urged him to run for sheriff. Most people thought he'd been a great game warden, and the fact he was now a city officer gave him even more credibility. And there was a feeling throughout the county that he had gotten a bum rap from the Conservation Department.

Herb Reynolds, the town's favorite professional photographer, gave Dad a great price on a campaign photo, and the new candidate headed to a print shop to have campaign cards printed. He also ordered some large posters: "Hallie Rowe for Sheriff." I was only ten but I hiked down to the dime store and purchased myself a small stapler. Then I walked the city, block-by-block, tacking a poster to every wooden street post I could find. There must have been a thousand of them.

Furnace Murder

I don't think the campaign cost Dad more than $300, all of which came from his own pocket. He wouldn't ask anyone for contributions, because he didn't want to be indebted to anyone if he won. On voting day he and Mom were first in line at the polling place, and when they returned home I mischievously asked Dad, "Did you vote for yourself?" His answer shocked me: "No, I left it blank." He could be modest but I couldn't believe he was telling the truth. What if he lost by one vote! That night we were all nervous but, as it turned out, it was wasted worry. Dad won by a landslide, garnishing more votes than his three opponents combined.

Before he took over as sheriff, however, there was one big job left for the Rowes, and it was especially painful for me. We had lived in our brand new house for only a little over two years and I loved everything about it—the mansion next door, looking out my front window, and all my neighborhood friends, including Zero before he died. But now it was all in the past. By year's end we rented our house and moved into the sheriff's residence at the jail.

~ ~ ~

On a cold day in late December 1944, the movers arrived at our house to pack up all of our earthly belongings and haul us to the county jail. With that I became a denizen of the immense, foreboding jail building. Imperceptibly— inextricably, really—my life took a new direction. I had done nothing wrong, but in a few short years I would lose my innocence, morphing from a ten-year-old boy into a jaded teenager.

The massive jail housed not only the current sheriff's family but also ghosts of sheriffs past. We would draw from their experiences, remember the incidents that had taken place there, and relate them to our future. Eventually I came to feel myself become a part of the jail itself. All the former sheriffs and their families, the police officers, and the inmates—all the triumphs and tragedies were seemingly absorbed by that somber structure.

It was an old building, completed in 1909 with stone from local quarries, and its dark, grey walls led to its nickname, "The Greystone Hotel." It was nothing like any hotel I'd ever been in. I don't recall much about the day Dad took me to meet his predecessor, Sheriff Brann, except that the residential quarters were off limits and there were solid steel doors and barred windows everywhere.

For years the jail building served as home for sheriffs and their families. The sheriff's wife was expected to cook meals for the prisoners, wash the jail laundry, and serve as receptionist in the jail office. No one told Mom that whenever Dad was absent, she was expected to serve as warden-in-charge. Mom was officially on the payroll, receiving thirty cents for each meal served to the prisoners and an even smaller amount for doing their washing.

When we were finally settled, Dad took me aside and set down several cardinal rules: First, I was never to trust a prisoner no matter how trustworthy he or she might seem to be. Second, the only persons coming in and out of the jail that I was to trust were the police officers. Third, the master jail keys were hidden, for security purposes, on a hook in a closet in the residential quarters, and I was never to tell *anyone,* not even the trusty police officers, where they were kept.

Finally, anything I heard or saw in the building was to "stay behind bars," as Dad phrased it. There would be no secrets shared with friends and absolutely no rumors repeated to anyone outside the family. He knew what I didn't—that I would be regularly exposed not only to aggressive prisoners who had to be physically restrained but also to the ferocious language that was certain to accompany these incidents. And my school friends would be dying to hear the juicy details.

The first few weeks of living in the jail were challenging, yet fascinating. A great new world opened to me, dwarfing my past experiences. I was fascinated by the heavy steel doors, the bars on the windows, the large spacious rooms, several of which had porches, the little pantry connecting the jail kitchen to the sheriff's personal dining room, and the long corridors and steep stairways.

I was assigned a private bedroom on the second floor of the living quarters, plus I had access to a storage room where I worked on my various projects. I was allowed to explore the expansive basement, which was divided into countless rooms. Perhaps most fascinating were the thick, steel-reinforced walls. Because prisoners were never allowed down there, I couldn't figure out the purposes of those mighty walls. I do know this: Any fool who rammed one of *those* walls with his head would be knocked out cold. Not that I ever tried it.

Also in that magical basement was a puzzling, small chamber without a door. It had only a small, barred window opening to the outside, but when I peered out with a flashlight I could see nothing at all. I imagined it to be our execution chamber. How exhilarating!

Directly above the basement was the cellblock where all the prisoners lived. I asked Dad endless questions like, Why were there thick metal bars on all the basement windows, and why was the door that led outside so heavily fortified? Dad was patient, even though in retrospect I realize how naïve my questions were. Using mostly hand gestures, he explained that on the floor just above us were dangerous prisoners itching to escape, and they would do anything to gain freedom, including burrowing a tunnel from their cells down into the basement.

Mom and Dad occupied the only bedroom on the first floor, the "master" bedroom. It had a little lavatory reserved for the personal use of the sheriff and his wife, though they let *me* use it once in a while. A telephone sat next to the bed for the inevitable trouble calls in the middle of the night. Typically the calls would come from one citizen complaining about another, just like kids. Dad always said that it was Mom who raised me, because he had his hands full parenting all the tattletales in town.

The public had a morbid curiosity about what was going on inside the jail. As they strolled or drove by, people would slow down and rubberneck, as though they expected a prisoner to escape at any moment. Knowing firsthand everything that was going on inside made me feel like a real celebrity.

The second-floor storeroom—my den—had a window that opened onto a porch directly above the jail kitchen. By crawling through this window and onto the porch, I could reach a metal stairway that allowed me to exit the building without being seen— except by the neighbors. They weren't used to seeing children escaping from the jail, and on several occasions they called Mom to rat me out. Luckily Mom seemed more peeved at the nosy neighbors than at me.

Rowe and Dodd

The dumbest thing I ever did at the jail had to do with the lighting. During Dad's first term in office, Mom had to be hospitalized for ten days for a goiter operation. While visiting at the hospital, I became intrigued by the red lights that showed the way at each of the many exits. Back home I asked myself, if the hospital can have red exit lights, why can't the jail? I spent a lot of time replacing dim yellow bulbs with bright red ones, and at night I went outside to admire my efforts. Dad was too busy with work and worried about Mom to even notice my modifications, until he got calls from neighbors complaining about the "inappropriate lighting."

I wasn't the only jail resident who got into a little trouble during Mom's hospitalization. A city police officer felt sorry for us, I guess, and brought us a couple of live chickens so that Mom would have something on hand to cook after she was discharged. Dad didn't know what to do with the chickens, so he turned them loose in the basement, where they roamed from room to room, clucking contently. When Mom got home she was shocked by not only the cluckers but also all the empty Pepsi bottles I had left behind while watching the chickens. Mom let Dad and me know right away who *really* ruled the roost.

The grounds around the building were spacious and we maintained them ourselves, with occasional help from the inmates. Our yard spilled right into the courthouse lawn, making for quite a playground. In the summer my friends and I sometimes set off the high-powered sprinklers and ran through them in our swimsuits. We were probably too old for such shenanigans but couldn't resist. That drew a lot of complaints from stuffy-shirts who thought is was improper decorum for a jail and courthouse.

On weekends, when all the courthouse workers were at home, I'd use Dad's master key and have the entire courthouse to myself. It was great fun prowling the hallways and dodging the custodian. In fact, I smoked my first cigarette in the spacious washroom in the basement. During the summer I often made regular social calls at the courthouse, going from office to office to greet elected officials and clerical workers by their first names. For the most part they were friendly and didn't seem to mind putting their work aside to chat with a kid.

Furnace Murder

~ ~ ~

In my four years living at the jail, I saw a lot of prisoners come and go. A few were big shots who considered themselves too important and influential to be arrested, but Dad didn't flinch when they tried to talk their way out of trouble. More often though, the inmates I saw were generally good people who made a mistake while down on their luck. Dad had a soft spot for most of them and had a knack for earning their trust with kindness, rather than going strictly by the book. It wasn't all charity on his part, though. Dad knew he could count on their help as informants on more serious cases down the road.

3

The Greystone Hotel

It was December 1945 and our first year as jail residents was coming to a close. It had been a spectacular year for me, exploring and taking in all the new sights and sounds. From my second-floor bedroom, I could even hear the songs from the loudspeaker at the city ice rink only a block away at Market Square.

It was the night bell at the jail, though, that thrilled me the most. Its ringing was Dad's signal to spring into action and mine to hop out of bed and sneak a peek at our newest prisoner. Dad first searched the criminal, then booked him, and finally hauled him off to the cellblock. I couldn't wait till breakfast to grill Dad for all the details.

We usually had a prisoner or two under our watch. We treated the men so well I'm sure a lot of them wanted to stay even after their time was up. Mom served them the very same meals Dad and I got—she didn't feel like keeping separate menus—so the inmates always looked forward to chow. At Christmas time Mom even included holiday cookies with meals to brighten their day.

Generally I liked having prisoners around, though they cramped my style. When the jail was empty I had free reign of the premises and could do my homework in any cell I wanted, though I had a favorite one. On weekends I'd ask a pal over for lunch and he chose which cell we ate in. I figured that *had* to help my popularity at school.

That first year we had 221 inmates pass in and out of jail, and I tried to keep a log of each one of them. I wrote down each name, date and time of booking, and the offense. It got to be way too much though, and I quit—I was only eleven! But I do recall that the most common charge was "drunk and disorderly." Whenever a repeat offender arrived, I could sense Dad groaning, but I was always glad to see an old friend again. I was on a first-name basis with many of them, and I think for some our jail was like home.

As any sheriff would, I suppose, Dad had a routine. At 10:00 each evening he made his rounds and locked the prisoners up in their individual cells. I doubt he tucked them in, because he'd stopped doing that with me years earlier. During the day he allowed inmates the freedom to wander around the first floor, especially during hot summer days, because it was so much cooler and the boys could use the exercise.

Most inmates really appreciated Dad's consideration, but on the evening of Labor Day 1945, we had a real incident. Two seasoned inmates, after monitoring Dad's routine for a few days, hatched an escape plot. Two steel doors, the second of which always remained unlocked, separated the jail office from the cellblock. That night Dad carelessly left the first door open and headed toward the second door, behind which the prisoners lay in wait. Just as Dad passed through, they shot out and slammed the door behind them, assuming incorrectly that the door would automatically lock, thus trapping the sheriff. But they miscalculated.

Upstairs I lay in bed, not yet asleep. In a bedroom next to mine was Uncle Herb, who was visiting for a few days. When the large steel door in the cellblock slammed shut, the noise reverberated throughout the jail. I sprang out of bed and yelled, "Come on, Uncle Herb. We got us a jailbreak!"

What a thrill! The escapees had figured they might have to contend with Mom and me, but they hadn't counted on Uncle Herb and his frame of more than 200 pounds. Thundering down the stairs we went—a combined 305 pounds. We caught up with the escapees just as they reached the exit door in the jail office, which to their surprise was bolted tight! Dad, Herb, and I all converged on the pair at once— we had them cornered and they gave up without a fight. Dad marched them right back to their cells, and you could tell he was none too happy.

Rowe and Dodd

At breakfast the next morning, Mom was so angry she served the inmates nothing but bread and water. Over that meager breakfast those two were feeling mighty sorry for themselves, but the worst was yet to come. A day later the circuit judge sentenced one to state prison and the other to the state reformatory.

Even on routine days there was always excitement. Once I found a bulletproof vest in storage and tried it on. It was too big but that didn't stop me from pestering a deputy to shoot me. Dad stopped that right away, though he did allow the deputy to punch me in the gut a couple of times.

One day I returned from school and found my parents and two police officers standing in the residential corridor, with windows everywhere wide-open. An undersheriff had stumbled upon a tear gas bomb in storage and was clowning around with it when it accidentally discharged. It was the kind of thing I might have been blamed for had I been home.

~ ~ ~

As tenants of Door County Jail, my family became, to a degree, inmates ourselves. We never took a vacation, not that we had even during Dad's sixteen years as game warden. Dad was never in favor of vacations—I guess nothing could compare to the excitement of law enforcement. I could see his point, in a way.

On occasion we did spend a night or even a weekend at the home of my Rowe grandparents in Wautoma, Wisconsin, about 130 miles from Sturgeon Bay. Mom's sister Ida and her husband also had a farm not far from there, so we got to visit both places in one trip. My folks always took a bushel or two of Door County apples to dole out to the relatives. Those apples filled the trunk of our car, and the combined odor of the apples and exhaust fumes always made me carsick—once I even threw up on the way. My parents weren't all that sympathetic, though. After that, they made sure I always had a barf bag, but they never stopped hauling apples to relatives.

~ ~ ~

Furnace Murder

I hated to see the end of the summer of 1946. There was always a lot of action going on at the jail, plus my friends and I had a ball antagonizing the courthouse custodian. Another reason I dreaded my return to school was that I was entering seventh grade, and for the first time I didn't know my teachers personally. Always before, my teachers had been friends of my parents, or I had somehow managed to ingratiate myself with them.

But the summer wasn't yet over, and there was still excitement to be had. In mid-August, Dad arrested a local nineteen-year-old, and a week later along came his eighteen-year-old partner. One had confessed to stealing a boat motor and the other had burglarized a gas station—whether they worked these jobs solo or in cahoots was immaterial. Both of the inmates were new to the jail but not to crime, having frequently clashed with the law. Now they were in custody, awaiting a gloomy future behind bars.

Soon they were joined in jail by an eighteen-year-old deserter from the military. I don't know why, but Dad assigned the three to adjoining cells. Maybe it was for convenience or maybe Dad, out of kindness, wanted to allow the young criminals a little companionship before they got shipped their separate ways.

How hot that summer had been! On really hot days Dad let inmates hang out the barred windows for a little air. The three teens availed themselves of this opportunity and soon after availed themselves of what was *outside* the windows—two teenaged girls who themselves were practiced in skirting the law. Their five minds sprung into action and within a couple of days the girls had smuggled in hacksaw blades. After the first night of sawing, the boys meticulously removed all of the metal dust and covered the sawed bars with soap, dyed black to hide their efforts.

Dad should have known something was up. Our last jailbreak attempt had been exactly a year before, on Labor Day night. Now it was Labor Day 1946. At 10:30 p.m. my parents retired to their bedroom next to the jail office. Four hours later they were awakened by strange noises coming from the cellblock. Dad told Mom to wait in the office while he snuck around to the jail section. The deserter—first from the army, now from jail—was quickly apprehended, but the two thieves stole away.

Instead of merely fleeing town, the boys got greedy. They swiped a car and then stopped to burglarize a gas station, taking time to eat chips and stuff candy bars into their pockets. This gave Dad plenty of time to alert officers and get them stationed at the west end of the only bridge leading out of town.

Back at the jail Mom and I were on the edge of our seats, following all the excitement on the police radio. The getaway car was traveling across the bridge at a high rate of speed, approaching the police wagon blocking the road. The rookie officer radioed Dad to ask if he should move the squad car. "Hell, no, you idiot! Leave the car but get the hell out of there!" I'd never heard Dad call an officer an idiot, but under the circumstances I forgave him.

Seconds later Mom and I heard the horrific crash with our own ears, even though it was eight blocks away. Minutes later Dad marched the two through the jail office and back to their cells. Days later they were headed to the state reformatory.

It was a thrilling end to my summer, plus we made news statewide. In the *Door County Advocate*, the lead story began: "Quick thinking on the part of Sheriff Hallie Rowe resulted in the quick capture of three youths who broke out of the county jail." The *Milwaukee Journal* quipped in their headline: "If Sheriff Snored Louder, Youths Would Be Free." The *Green Bay Press-Gazette* sub-headed its story: "Sheriff is aroused when fat boy gets stuck in window, has right hunch in blocking bridge."

A month later I myself became a law enforcement officer, of sorts, even though I was only in seventh grade. Assistant Police Chief Romy Londo organized the first school safety patrol and began recruiting his understudies. I was already friends with Romy—sometimes we'd read comic books together at the jail— and when he personally asked me to join, I jumped at the chance. So there my friends and I were, with our armbands, official badges, and stop signs, ready to assist little kids across the busy intersections at noon. How hard could that be?

Furnace Murder

My first day on the job I stood in the middle of the intersection, holding my stop sign high. An older youth named Wilbur—a real rascal by everyone's account—ignored me and my sign and drove his car right through the intersection! I chased after him, yelling, "Wilbur went through! Wilber went through!" I was so mad, I think if I'd had a service revolver, I would have used it!

I was shocked when the teacher on playground duty reprimanded *me*, saying that I should have "handled the situation differently." Initially I just bit my tongue and took it, but by the end of my shift I was so mad I turned in my badge and stop sign and quit. I expected Romy to give the teacher a good bawling out and beg me to rejoin. Instead he merely complained to Dad that I had been the very first member of his patrol to quit.

I didn't know it at the time, but the crossing-guard incident changed me. Prior to seventh grade, I got good grades and positive checks on my report card for areas like conduct and, my favorite, "punctuality." But now my grades were slipping and my positive checks were being replaced by negative ones.

I was really astounded when I discovered one of my teachers marked me down for "lack of self-control." What nerve! Thinking back, though, I'm surprised I didn't also get checked for "lacks respect for authority," because that's exactly what was happening, real fast. There was an undercurrent in my life that was transforming me from a happy, cooperative little boy into an antagonistic teenager. When I thought back to those three teens who tried to escape jail, I even found myself feeling admiration for them. School was my jail and I could identify with the impulse of wanting to break free. My teachers—guards—were telling me what to do, where to sit, when to talk, and when to shut up. I was just another inmate.

One day at the end of seventh grade, my homeroom teacher had me stand and tell the class what it was like living in the county jail. She gave me fifteen minutes, including questions after my speech. I described the entire jail building and told about being privy to police secrets that I could never tell my friends and classmates. Then I told about some of the inmates—being careful not to call them by name—the drunks, the violent ones, and even the insane, who sometimes

Rowe and Dodd

ranted and raved and claimed to see snakes. And I told about all the crafty inmates who naively tried to fool Sheriff Rowe but never could. Though it was harder to do, I even tried to describe the bitterness and hate that are an integral part of the jail environment. And I told of the wives who cried while talking with their husbands through the bars, and the children who couldn't understand why their daddies were locked up.

It was impossible to tell it all in fifteen minutes, and my teacher cut me off abruptly at twenty minutes. I had done my best. At age thirteen I thought I had seen it all. But I really hadn't—the worst was yet to come.

4

Shopping

Dad faced re-election in 1946, but he had no opposition and breezed to victory. Most people were willing to give a sheriff "a second chance," barring broad malfeasance during the first term. On the other hand, term limits meant that would be it, so January 1947 marked the beginning of our final two years of residence at the jail.

I was still in seventh grade and was neck-deep in the usual school traumas. I was miserable and focused much more on my resentment and embarrassment than on math and English. Outside of school I was developing into a compulsive shopper, heading downtown every weekend to spend hours pouring over merchandise. Eventually I'd make my selection and head home with some crazy new acquisition. More times than not, my parents sent me straight back for a refund, often calling the storeowner in advance. Back into the store I'd go, my head hanging in embarrassment, and dang if the clerk wouldn't have a knowing grin on his face. I wanted to slap him but I figured he'd just call the law.

Sometimes my awkwardness reared its ugly head even at home. Once Dad ordered me to retrieve the master jail keys while he was booking in a new prisoner. Afterwards he reminded me to return the keys to their secret location but instead I just pocketed them, figuring I'd put them back later. Of course I forgot all about them and headed out for a shopping spree. When I walked into the Gamble store, I was immediately apprehended. Dad had already called to direct them to send me right home with the keys. On my way home I could tell from the reactions of store workers all along the way that it had not just been Gamble that Dad had called.

31

Rowe and Dodd

Dad tried to rehabilitate me by assigning me various chores around the jail, and some of them were actually very interesting. It was my responsibility to keep the large, cork bulletin board updated. Everyday I'd check the mail for capture announcements and dutifully mark "canceled" on the old notices. My style was to leave the canceled ones up until space was absolutely needed, so the board was always jammed full, thus making business look brisker than it actually was. Occasionally large posters of the FBI's "most wanted" came, and they were always the crown jewels of the bulletin board, drawing in quite a few impressionable townspeople. It was great—the jail office was a museum and I was the curator.

Another job of mine was to monitor the mail to and from the prisoners. For security reasons prisoners weren't allowed to seal their outgoing letters, and we opened incoming letters as well. Dad really showed confidence in me by giving me such an important responsibility—he knew I was a really good reader. But sometimes I spent way too much time pouring over those private letters, sniffing out details that really weren't any of my business.

During visiting hours I sat in the jail office overseeing visitors as they talked with prisoners through the barred window of the large, steel door leading back to the cellblock. I was on constant alert, observing every movement of both the visitor and the prisoner, especially their hands, so that nothing could be passed through the bars. I also timed the visits—otherwise those visitors would never leave. When they went too far over the fifteen-minute limit, I'd announce in my deepest voice, *Time to wrap it up. And make it snappy!* I wasn't all business, though. Sometimes I'd recognize a visitor from screening letters, and if I felt sorry enough for them, I'd give them a couple of extra minutes.

I'm sure I saved the county a lot of money by doing all those jobs, and in a way I even helped the local economy. Dad didn't pay me for my work but he was real good about slipping me cash all the time. He really enabled my shopping addiction.

When I was almost thirteen, Dad decided that I was old enough to see firsthand where some of the prisoners went after being sentenced. This gave me opportunities few kids my age ever had—touring most of the state's institutions, ranging from mental hospitals to maximum security prisons. The highlight of all those trips was visiting Waupun State Prison. Even though it was maximum security, we got the deluxe tour, since Dad knew the warden. On the way home Dad told me something that really surprised me. Before he became a game warden, he had been a tower guard at Waupun, with sharpshooter status!

One time Dad arrested a thirty-six-year-old man and charged him with rape. The man maintained his innocence, pleaded not guilty, and retained counsel. At the time authorities were just beginning to experiment with truth serum. The defendant's attorney, sure that it would provide exonerating evidence, asked that his client be allowed to be examined by professionals using the serum. The prosecution consented.

Off we went to Bradley Hospital in Madison. I wasn't permitted to witness the actual procedure and was very disappointed, though I didn't complain—I was lucky just to be there. Things didn't go as the man's attorney, or anyone else, had intended. The doctor administering the drug accidentally overdosed the man, who went into convulsions and nearly died.

Finally his vital signs stabilized and the questioning resumed. Whether it was because his answers were convincing or just that everyone was so shaken up by the overdose, it's hard to say, but the results were ruled "inconclusive." Dad himself was quite disturbed by the whole affair and let his feelings be known at the hospital. He was mighty quiet on the ride home—I think he felt fortunate to be returning to Sturgeon Bay with a live prisoner rather than a dead one. Later he recommended the rape charge be dropped, and it was.

~ ~ ~

It was January 1948 and Dad's four-year run as sheriff was nearing the final curtain. But he would be only fifty-two at year's end and had no idea what to do next with his life. Financially it was all unsettling, because at the time there wasn't even a pension for sheriffs.

Rowe and Dodd

The year started slowly. With time on his hands, Dad threw himself into the chore of tracking down husbands who had deserted their families. He couldn't stand the thought that these men would just take off, so he vowed to chase down the scoundrels and bring them back to Door County to face felony charges of non-support. Other officials marveled at his ability, especially when he was able to nab suspects who had cut off all local ties and fled to other states. Time after time he'd track them down, have the local sheriffs lock them up, and then take off to claim them and bring them back for justice.

Dad never revealed his strategy to anyone but Mom and me, and as usual we were sworn to secrecy. For years I never squealed but here goes: Dad's contact was an administrator in a regional Social Security office, who could have lost his job for divulging the information. But he was on Dad's side and trusted that he wouldn't get caught. It was a simple plan, really. Dad would just telephone his informant, and a few days later he had the suspect's employer and work address. Then he'd call the local sheriff and have the man apprehended. Off Dad would go, usually by car but sometimes by train, to retrieve his prey.

While Dad was off apprehending criminals, I was back at school in eighth grade, which I enjoyed even less than seventh. My school attitude was still lousy—basically my growing alienation just swallowed up any other emotions I might have had. More and more I found myself compelled to rebel, and I began to look suspiciously upon anyone who was not my steadfast friend—in other words, almost everyone. I didn't realize it at the time but all my experience in jail had hardened me.

Our homeroom teacher told us on the first day of class how tough he was. "I can take on any four of you at once," he bragged. I immediately tried to round up three buddies to prove the teacher wrong but could never get a commitment from more than one at a time.

Our English teacher naively tried to teach us language and grammar. He was deficient in a lot of ways but his biggest problem was a total lack of humor—everything was *so* serious. One day our class met in the science room, I can't remember why. He was running very late for class, so we troublemakers leaped into action. Scattered around the room were a dozen alarm clocks used to time experiments. We set them to ring a few minutes apart and hid them everywhere—in drawers, cabinets, and even right under the teacher's desk. Surprisingly the girls even joined in on the conspiracy, inflating balloons and hiding them under their desks.

When the teacher finally arrived, he must have been very impressed at how quiet and obedient we were being, as we attentively followed his movements at the front of the class. Soon he began reciting Longfellow: "I shot an arrow into the air." Immediately an alarm clock went off. Assuming it had been left over from a previous science class, the teacher located and silenced it. "It fell to earth I know not where." A balloon popped. Trying to ignore it, he continued. By the time he hit the third stanza, the class was total chaos. That day in class was the highlight of my entire eighth-grade year!

At about the same time that year, I was being prepped for confirmation at St. Peter's Lutheran Church. There, under the guidance of a very patient pastor, I was getting on much better than at school. Mom was active in the church and especially proud that I was being confirmed. Part of the ceremony was Communion, which to us kids mostly meant getting to drink wine. We couldn't wait!

~ ~ ~

Confirmation came and went that spring. I remember very little about it, except that they gave us only miniscule portions of wine, not nearly enough for any of us twerps to get drunk on. Just around the corner, though, was a crime I would never forget, and neither would any other adult, child, or sullen teenager living in Door County at the time. And the case would make my dad famous.

Part II

5

Mansion on Silk Stocking Hill

Sadie Marsh Cody stood on the sidewalk in front of her home at 12 North Church Street, listening to the ringing of distant church bells. The bells were from the west, across the bay that divided the town. She was glad she lived on the east side, and proud of her residence in the best neighborhood in town. Her mind carried her back to 1887, when she arrived in Sturgeon Bay as a young schoolteacher, full of ambition and dreams. Not in her wildest fantasy had she imagined being married to the town's most prominent man, a respected attorney and land broker.

Their lives were blessed. Just a year before their marriage, her husband Richard had purchased for $1000 a large tract of land that took up most of a city block. The sizable house that came with the land suited their purposes splendidly, but by 1903 they had even bigger ideas. They would build an elegant Victorian mansion that would be the grandest home in town.

It was now 1904, and they had been living in the mansion for only a few months. They had a brand new car in their garage. Irene, their only child, was a bright and popular fifteen-year-old with boundless energy and a bright future, Sadie was sure. The Codys had it all—what could possibly go wrong?

~ ~ ~

Richard P. Cody was born in Ireland in 1851, and just three months after his birth his family immigrated to America and settled on a farm near Manitowoc, Wisconsin. Eventually they moved to Oshkosh, where Richard graduated high school. He taught school for six years, but the job did not satisfy his financial aspirations, so he changed course. He went to law school, served an apprenticeship, was admitted to the state bar, and moved to Sturgeon Bay, where he began practicing law in 1881.

In a few short years, he had acquired vast land holdings and was gradually becoming one of the county's wealthiest citizens. He was even appointed district attorney. But as he reached his mid-thirties, he often felt weary from his feverish work habits. Richard was ready to settle down and start a family.

Fate drew Sadie Marsh into the divine orbit of Richard Cody. At least, that's what Sadie thought when she learned how much they had in common. They shared an Irish heritage. She was born in Sheboygan, a town not far from Richard's boyhood farm. Her father was a farmer, just like Richard's. Her family moved to Oshkosh, just as his had. Like Richard, she pursued a career as a teacher—a high-school education was the only requirement needed. Unlike Richard, though, she loved teaching and sought to excel. After a few years in the classroom, she sought additional training by enrolling in the Oshkosh Normal School, the same school Richard attended before becoming a lawyer. The two seemed destined for each other.

In 1887 Sadie learned of a teaching position at Sturgeon Bay, ninety miles from Oshkosh. She applied and was quickly hired, much to her delight. The starting salary of $40 per month was enough to support herself and still send some money home to her parents. At the young age of twenty-five, Sadie was happy in her new life and proud of her self-sufficiency.

Not long after she arrived in town, Sadie met Richard. Almost immediately, they began seeing each other everyday, and their time together provided him a much needed diversion from the demands of his career. It was a perfect match. He was attracted to her charm, quick wit, keen mind, and fashionable attire—plus Sadie had a profession. A former teacher himself, Richard admired her skill and enthusiasm and enjoyed hearing her daily accounts of classroom activities, especially the tales of students' misbehavior. And she was well aware that Richard was the town's most eligible bachelor.

After a whirlwind romance, the two were ready for marriage, waiting only for the 1887–88 school term to end. Sadie loved teaching but gladly gave it up to marry Richard. Despite her exuberant nature, Sadie had a private side and did not want an ostentatious wedding in Sturgeon Bay. Instead they had a quiet ceremony at her parents' home. It had been a storybook romance, and taking Richard home to Oshkosh was Sadie's way of sharing her success with her parents, who had always struggled against poverty. Sadie Marsh was now Mrs. Richard Cody, the wife of Sturgeon Bay's most prominent citizen.

Within two months Sadie became pregnant, and the following April, the couple celebrated the birth of little Irene. Marriage ended Sadie's teaching career, but if she felt any void, motherhood filled it. The joy of caring for Irene overshadowed even her active social life and community involvement. But at the turn of the century, Irene turned eleven and was starting to become more independent. Sadie began to immerse herself once again in civic life.

At the time, wives were expected to be subordinate to their husbands, but the Codys did not follow this norm. Sadie independently supported a variety of worthy causes, some of which the image-conscious Richard would not touch. For example, in 1903 Sadie affixed her name along with others, mostly women, to newspaper advertisements urging local merchants to observe earlier closing hours for their stores. Long working hours deprived employees of time with their wives and children, and the petition called for uniform store closings by 6:00 p.m. The action was not entirely successful but did result in a more relaxed closing policy by many establishments. As a lawyer and banker who dealt daily with merchants, Richard understandably chose to avoid the controversy.

"Mrs. Richard Cody" had a more important calling than mere chores at home. The family could afford to hire as much help as needed, freeing Sadie to explore her diverse interests. Always fastidious and exquisitely dressed, Sadie cultivated a prominence of her own. She commanded respect and generally got it—gentlemen would tip their hats as she passed by.

Rowe and Dodd

In 1904 personal automobiles were just becoming available and the Codys, of course, were among the first in town to purchase one. Sadie was one of the first women drivers, but as she was learning she ran into a little trouble —actually, it was a pedestrian! Fortunately the victim was not seriously injured. As an apology, Sadie bought the man a box of chocolate candy, a small gesture that appeased the man and kept the story out of the newspapers.

The Codys took pride in their reputation for honesty, virtue, and respectability, traits they deliberately groomed in their daughter. They contributed generously to education and other worthy causes in the church and community. Sadie enjoyed teaching Sunday school at Hope Congregational Church and especially liked working with the little children in her class.

Bright and friendly, Irene Cody was popular at school and in the community. Like her mother, Irene was inquisitive, intelligent, and vivacious, with a flair for fashion. A local publication described her as "a maiden who is cute, modest, and most sincere." Despite the accolades, Irene was proudest of serving as editor of her school newsletter.

In just a few short years, Irene would be leaving home for college and a career of her own. Though thrilled for her daughter, Sadie was saddened by the prospects of an empty nest, so she hatched a plan and presented it to Richard. She recognized that they already had a beautiful house in the best part of town, but why not build something even grander? They certainly had the finances to do it, and a mansion would guarantee their status in the community. They had given Irene the best of everything. Now they would treat themselves to a dream of their own.

Everything inside and out would reflect the proper decor of great mansions, and Sadie hoped that it would become their family legacy. Far into the future it would represent the prominence of their family in Sturgeon Bay. And there was even a practical matter to consider: Irene would undoubtedly marry and return with a family of her own for extended visits. Grandchildren would romp throughout the great house, calling out delightfully for Grandma.

Furnace Murder

By January 1904, after six months of construction, the mansion was finally ready for the Codys to move in. Final touches were completed in March, and rave reviews began shortly thereafter. One local newspaper described it as "an elegant residence which is one of the most complete in all its details to be seen in this part of the state." As the days grew warmer that spring, more and more people from far and near came to admire the mansion—a "must see" for out-of-town visitors and residents alike. The Codys even opened their residence for public tours!

Visitors bragged about being inside and described in detail the opulence they witnessed. The elaborate woodwork was hand-carved and bathrooms were furnished with special marble washbowls and unique faucets. Windows with panels of colored glass were plentiful. Electric lighting, a rarity for private residences at the time, brightened every floor. A tower rising high above the rambling front porch broadcasted the expansiveness of the mansion.

Proud as they were of the final product, Richard and Sadie were relieved that the project was finally completed. The many months of construction had taken its toll, and Sadie could not stop reliving an incident that nearly cost a worker his life. Plans called for the most modern heating system available—steam-heating fueled by a large coal-burning furnace in the cellar. Extremely heavy, bulky radiators had to be installed in every room throughout the mansion. One morning as workers were carrying a radiator through a rear door, the back porch gave way and the radiator crushed several men, nearly killing one of them.

Although the worker eventually recovered, Sadie was devastated by the accident and irrationally placed the blame upon the furnace. In future years, whenever it roared into action and began circulating heat throughout the mansion, Sadie shuddered as she recalled the nearly fatal accident. There was something sinister about the fiery furnace in the spooky cellar, she felt.

~ ~ ~

Sadie was so proud of her creation—when people stopped to admire the mansion, she delighted in making conversation and elaborating on every little detail. She showed off her prized new home by hosting numerous parties, especially card parties, which local newspapers typically noted, "Mrs. R.P. Cody entertained a score of ladies at Cinch on Thursday afternoon at her beautiful new home on Church Street."

Mesmerized by her new home, Sadie loved and nurtured it during every moment of its "infancy." Though her pragmatic husband scoffed at the notion, she believed the mansion was her "child"—hers forever to care for, enjoy, and protect. And unlike a child who would eventually leave her, the mansion would always be hers.

Their grand home was a symbol of their past success and their bright future. Unfortunately though, clouds were on the horizon. By the end of April, Richard became ill with pleurisy and was confined to bed for a week. Tending her husband reminded Sadie of another impending problem—the needs of her aging mother Emily. She had been alone in Oshkosh since her husband's death in 1897, and now her own health was rapidly deteriorating. By summer of 1905, it was agreed that Emily would come to live at the mansion, where she could be properly cared for. It was a good arrangement but lasted only seven months. By the end of the year, Sadie's mother was dead at age seventy-six, the official cause of death reported as "senility."

Within weeks of her mother's death, Richard again became ill and was confined to the mansion under doctor's orders. Sadie was particularly distressed, since her husband's illness so closely followed the strain of caring for her dying mother. A visit from her longtime friend and confidante, Mrs. George Spear of Green Bay, buoyed Sadie. Louise spent a week at the mansion, assisting Sadie and giving her time to relax. Over the next few months, Richard recovered and resumed his demanding law practice, though there were occasional relapses.

The next big event in the family was Irene's high school graduation at the end of June 1906. The occasion was joyously celebrated at the mansion, and everyone was excited about Irene's enrollment in the University of Wisconsin at Madison in the fall. After enduring the death of Sadie's mother and Richard's lingering illness, surely the Codys were staging a comeback.

Furnace Murder

But Irene's departure to attend the university left a void in the lives of her parents. Richard coped by pushing himself even harder at his work, despite days when his illness got the best of him. Though she tried to stay involved with church and social activities, Sadie spent more and more time at the mansion, tending to him and worrying constantly. Once frequent travels to visit friends and relatives ground to a halt.

Irene returned home for a ten-day visit at Thanksgiving and again at Christmas, the latter time accompanied by a classmate. Both girls were residing on campus at the exclusive Chadbourn Hall. Several days prior to their departure from campus, a hall resident contracted smallpox. University officials first considered quarantining everyone but instead merely required everyone to be vaccinated before leaving campus.

After Christmas, Sadie held a dinner party for the children from her Sunday school class. It was her holiday present to her pupils, and they were thrilled to be invited to the Cody mansion. The party was one of the last truly happy events in the life of Sadie Cody.

~ ~ ~

Twilight came early in those cold days of winter, and the darkness of night seemed to foreshadow the blackness that was preparing to descend upon the Codys. Irene was back at the university now, and Sadie missed her deeply. Furthermore, Richard's almost obsessive need to achieve was taking over. Though it was hard for him to get to the office on a daily basis, he could not let go. The Cody image of prominence and prosperity was at stake.

Richard's illness was very hard on Sadie. She did her best to comfort him and, when she couldn't, worried herself sick. Louise Spear again came to stay for a week to fortify her friend and lessen the burden. Sadie reciprocated in the way she knew best—by throwing a party in Louise's honor.

When Louise's visit ended, though, a gnawing feeling returned. As her husband lay in his second floor bedroom, Sadie could only pray that rest would restore his failing health. Two days later, a specialist from Chicago arrived to examine him, with grim results. Richard was suffering from cancer of the throat and the prognosis was bleak. Sadie felt doomed but Richard almost irrationally anticipated a quick recovery and a return to his business activities.

Sadie sent word to Richard's brother Joseph, who arrived in January 1908 to assess the situation. A local newspaper splashed Richard's illness across its front pages, and the family was not pleased. It promptly persuaded another newspaper, the *Democrat*, to publish a more favorable view: "Richard Cody is said to be slowly gaining strength." But Richard was not improving. For the entire month of February, he lay dying. Still, he insisted on running his business advertisements in each issue of the local newspapers.

On the first day of March, a death watch began. Richard's good friend W.J. Turner of Milwaukee came to pay him a final visit. Cody had begun the practice of law with Turner's firm in Manitowoc, and now it was time for the two good friends to say goodbye. The next day Irene came home from Madison to be at her father's side.

On March 4, Richard Cody died in his bedroom at the mansion. News spread quickly throughout the city, and flags were lowered to half-mast, including the one at the schoolhouse only a half block away from the mansion. Sturgeon Bay's most prominent citizen was dead.

The following morning, the schoolhouse, with its flag still at half-mast, burned to the ground. The early morning blaze could be seen for blocks, and it silhouetted the nearby Cody mansion. The school had been a second home to generations of children from kindergarten through senior high. For many years Richard Cody had reigned over the schoolhouse as president of the school board. Now both were gone.

While the school fire still raged just down the street, Sadie and Irene headed dutifully to Bayside Cemetery to secure a burial plot for Richard. They sensibly chose a plot spacious enough for all three Codys, plus any grandchildren that might follow. And they crossed their fingers that Richard would rest *alone* for many years to come.

At Richard's burial Sadie stood at her husband's gravesite, paralyzed. For the first time in her adult life, she did not know what to do. She thought back to just four years earlier. The completion of the mansion thrilled the Cody family and seemed to represent a bright horizon. Now it was the schoolhouse, smoldering in ashes, that symbolized the future. At age forty-six, Sadie was too young to give up but too old to start over. It was only her love for Irene that sustained her, and she prayed for her daughter's happiness and future.

6

Valley of Death

The last rites for Richard Cody were pronounced at Bayside Cemetery. Sadie Cody turned and walked away from her husband's cold grave, overwhelmed not only by grief but fear. All her beautiful memories of times with Richard were now painful, their plans for the future shattered. What lay ahead?

When Sadie arrived back at the mansion, the pungent smell of charred wood was still rising from the smoldering schoolhouse. It was a stark reminder of her youthful past—when she had moved to Sturgeon Bay to begin her teaching career in that very building and ended up meeting and marrying Richard. Her thoughts then turned to those horrible months her mother lay dying in the mansion.

Built as a symbol of grandeur and happiness, the mansion had instead become a place of despair. First her mother died there, now Richard. All that she had left was her daughter, who was rapidly becoming a beautiful, independent adult. Oh, for the days when Irene was growing up and all of her young friends came to visit, the mansion always abuzz with youthful activity. And Richard's comings and goings—how she missed their exciting conversations about his financial successes. All of it was gone now.

Soon Irene would leave the gloomy mansion to return to the university. Surely she would marry and have children, but would she ever return to live in Sturgeon Bay? Sadie couldn't stand the prospect of being alone.

At least she still had her best friend Louise Spear, who had been there to support Sadie through the illnesses and deaths of her mother and husband. Louise knew just what to say—and when to say it—

whenever grief was about to drown Sadie. And hearing her friend refer to her as "Sadie" warmed her heart. To everyone else, she was "Mrs. Cody." Before long she would be called "Widow Cody," she fretted.

Many times over the years prior to Richard's death, Sadie made the forty-two mile trip to stay with Louise at her magnificent home, within walking distance of the thriving business district of Green Bay. There she and Louise would spend hours shopping in fashionable stores, stopping only for lunch at an upscale restaurant. Like Sadie, Louise was civic-minded and belonged to several social clubs. The two were movers and shakers in their respective communities, and the visits between the "grande dames" were always duly noted in the newspapers.

Memories of those wonderful days gave way to the reality of the moment and all of her self-doubts. Could she have done more during the months that Richard's health was failing? What if she had contacted a specialist sooner? By the time the specialist from Chicago arrived, it had been too late. Why couldn't there have been a doctor right in Sturgeon Bay to properly diagnose and treat Richard's disease? Instead, they had been forced to rely on the familiar, local general practitioners, who obviously were unqualified to handle something like cancer. Sadie was sick with self-blame.

Irene was painfully aware of her mother's suffering, but there was little she could do. Her mother wanted her to return to the university and pursue her own future, and she herself wanted that too. But Irene sensed what might lie around the corner. Her father had amassed a fortune through his law practice and business ventures, and now his wife was the richest widow in town. Irene worried that her lonely, grieving mother would be vulnerable to those wanting to take advantage of her.

Sadie and her daughter made a joint decision. Irene would not return to the university immediately. Instead she would stay in Sturgeon Bay and together they would protect the family's financial interests. A *team*, they would grieve together, bolster each other, and set the sails of the Cody financial ship.

Keeping her mother active and away from the mansion as much as possible became Irene's most immediate goal. Mother loved to travel, she knew, so Irene accompanied her at the end of March to Marinette, Wisconsin, for an extended visit with relatives. Then after spending the early summer in Sturgeon Bay, Sadie and Irene set out again, this time visiting friends and relatives in Oshkosh, Manitowoc, and other stops along the way.

Irene felt pleased to be keeping her mother busy and occupied, with little time to dwell on her misfortunes. Finally, Sadie's grief seemed to wane and she began managing her financial affairs on her own. In March 1909, Irene returned to her studies at the University of Wisconsin, though she returned a few weeks later with a classmate for an extended Easter break. Six weeks later Sadie embarked on another trip to visit friends and relatives. In late June she picked up Irene in Madison and the two returned to Sturgeon Bay.

As the second anniversary of Richard's death approached, Sadie continued to grieve quietly. Gradually though, she began to assume a more active role in the community. This is what Richard would have wanted—for her to be strong and assertive. It was up to her to attend to the financial dealings, so the empire he had worked so hard to build would not collapse. Eerily Sadie felt Richard's presence, as though he were helping her. Together they would realize their family dreams. And Sadie would insist that Irene put herself first, complete college, begin a career, and have a family.

Maintaining the mansion and restoring her image in the community became Sadie's calling. It had been two long years since Richard's death. Throughout that time she often looked out her west window and watched as the new schoolhouse was being constructed on the site of the old one. If the town could rebuild a school, she could rebuild her life. It was time to stop grieving and get on with her future.

~ ~ ~

In 1910 Sadie burst forth with a new exuberance, as if to make up for lost time. She was determined to put to rest the town's image of her as the grieving Widow Cody. She met with her personal attorney and informed him that there were numerous payments long overdue on real estate mortgages and other obligations. Many of the individuals to whom Richard had loaned substantial amounts of money had simply stopped making payments. Sadie was adamant that legal proceedings begin as a warning that no one could default on their Cody loans.

As a number of legal actions began making their way through the courts, many people accused Sadie of becoming too assertive. In the past Richard had initiated the legal maneuvers, and townspeople expected no less from such an ultimate entrepreneur. The fact that Sadie Cody was exhibiting the same financial shrewdness riled many people, especially those who were losing to her in court.

Sadie was also reemerging socially and entertaining regularly at the mansion. For example, she hosted a Progressive Rummy party in honor of Louise Spear. A few weeks later she met Louise and other friends for a week in Green Bay. In mid-September Sadie accompanied Irene to Madison in preparation for the fall term at the university.

After returning from Madison, Sadie hosted a succession of social events. The *Door County Advocate* reported, for example, "Mrs. R.P. Cody entertained about twenty ladies at her beautiful home on Church Street. Progressive Bridge Whist was played, and after cards the hostess took her guests to the Catholic Fair Supper where a table had been reserved."

While Sadie and friends were enjoying a carefree day, an event with truly sinister ramifications was taking place, unnoticed. Elmer H. Robb, M.D., a widower, moved to Sturgeon Bay. He had been practicing medicine for almost a year on Washington Island at the northern tip of county, sixty miles away. Now he was locating his new office right downtown. A local newspaper devoted an entire story to the doctor, noting, "He has purchased a part of an estate in the Third District of Sevastopol and will combine the practice of his profession with that of fruit growing. A well developed cherry orchard already stands on the premises."

Seven months later Dr. Robb relocated his residence to upper Cottage Street, a mere two blocks from the Cody mansion. He was no longer interested in harvesting merely fruit. Sadie Cody was his target.

7

Good Night, Irene

During the Christmas holidays of 1910, Irene had plenty of time to talk with her mother. She was concerned how rapidly Sadie transforming herself from a weary, depressed woman into a demanding, self-assured businesswoman. It was all too quick for comfort. Certainly it was wrong that debtors were ignoring their obligations to the estate, just because they assumed a woman would be too timid to challenge them in court. And the family attorney was providing the legal muster to Sadie's financial maneuvers. Still, Irene was worried, and she decided to intervene.

Sadie listened intently as Irene expressed her concerns. Why go it alone? There was Henry Fetzer at the bank, a trusted friend who could be forceful without arousing the antagonism that a woman of that day would when she asserted herself. Ask him for his assistance, Irene begged, and Sadie was receptive. Soon a meeting with the banker was set. Fetzer agreed to assist with the affairs of the sizable Cody estate, and a new firm of Cody and Fetzer was even established.

As Irene headed back to the university following the holiday break, everything seemed on track. Emulating her driven father, Irene pushed herself hard to succeed, studying feverishly and earning top grades. She also strove for excellence in her extracurricular endeavors, winning second place in a university oratorical contest for her oration titled "Call to the Soil." Sadie was extremely proud of Irene's award and made sure it was announced in the local newspaper.

In January 1911, the first announcement for Cody and Fetzer appeared in the newspaper, advertising that it had "money to lend." Ironically, the notice appeared in the same place where Richard Cody's ads had always been displayed. Almost eerily, Dr. E.H. Robb's announcement of the location of his new office appeared adjacent to Sadie's.

Meanwhile Dr. Robb's short morning walk from his home to office took him within a half block of the Cody mansion. He kept his eyes out for Mrs. Cody, and if he spotted her he'd tip his hat. Soon he was taking a short detour that almost assured face-to-face encounters with her. Sure enough, simple greetings soon turned into short conversations, and within days their daily exchanges expanded from seconds to minutes.

Just prior to the conclusion of Irene's spring semester in June, Sadie received a disturbing telephone call. The university dean announced that Irene was seriously ill and advised Sadie to come to Madison immediately. She hurriedly put everything aside and made the long drive that very day. There she found Irene weak and lethargic, in need of intensive care. Characteristically though, Irene insisted on staying to complete her semester requirements, and amazingly she was able to do so. It all reminded Sadie of how Richard would slowly rise from his bed at the mansion, put in a full day's work, and return home, wracked in pain. It also brought to mind her greatest regret in life—that she had not insisted upon hiring a specialist who could correctly diagnose Richard's cancer.

She would not repeat the mistake with her daughter. More than one highly qualified doctor was consulted, and the consensus was awful—Irene had tuberculosis. At the time, specialists could diagnose the disease but knew virtually nothing about its cause or effective treatment. The prescription was simple: complete rest in a place with abundant fresh air.

Sadie and Irene discussed the situation thoroughly. Sadie vowed that her daughter would receive the very best of care—they could afford it and Irene would get it. She would enter the River Pines Sanatorium at Stevens Point, which specialized in treating tuberculosis. There she would recuperate in relative comfort. On her first visit to the sanatorium, Sadie made Irene promise to get well again, and the daughter solemnly vowed to. It was a ritual the two would enact repeatedly over the next several months.

Back in Sturgeon Bay, Sadie made a point of talking to Dr. Elmer Robb about Irene's situation, hoping he could shed light on everything. She had little confidence in the other doctors in town, given their failure to help Richard, but maybe a new doctor could help. Though Robb had no special knowledge of tuberculosis, she was encouraged by his offer to assist in any way possible. Placing Irene at the sanatorium was absolutely the correct decision, Robb assured her. Sadie was grateful for his attention and admired his expertise.

An opportunist, Robb quickly recognized that Sadie was a woman in distress—and a very wealthy one at that. Calculations swirled in his mind. He kept secret his belief that Irene would die before ever returning to the mansion. Without her daughter, Sadie would be alone in the world and inevitably open her arms to his friendship. All kinds of opportunities might arise. Robb kept reassuring her that she was doing the wise thing by placing Irene in the hands of the caring specialists at the sanatorium. And he politely offered to assist Sadie in anyway he could.

That summer Sadie kept in close touch with Irene through letters and periodic visits to Stevens Point. Occasionally she would even call her daughter on the telephone, though she was uncomfortable with the cost of long-distance calls. At the end of August, Louise Spear persuaded the weary Sadie to visit, and the two friends spent several days together, especially enjoying a day at the Brown County Fair in DePere. When she returned home, though, Sadie was once again beset by loneliness and anxiety. Would her daughter ever get well?

In early November, encouraging news finally came in. Irene was on the mend and her doctors indicated she could return home by Christmas. Sadie was elated and immediately began decorating. Once again the mansion would be full of holiday joy, she envisioned.

But the doctors were wrong. Irene was not improving, instead her condition was worsening. Sadie's Christmas would be spent with Irene at the sanatorium. It was such a lonely place—most residents had gone home for family visits and few staff remained on duty. But at least the Cody family of two was together.

Furnace Murder

After Christmas, Sadie returned home a troubled woman, antici-
pating the worst. Her spirits were battered not only by Irene's setback
but also by brutal weather. January was a month of bitterly cold, with
record-setting temperatures reaching thirty-two degrees below zero.
The coal-burning furnace in the cellar did its best to warm the mansion, but what Sadie needed most was human warmth.

With increasing regularity Elmer Robb dropped in to visit, always
with fawning inquiries about Irene. After offering concern and words
of wisdom, he quickly turned the conversation to current events.
Naturally inquisitive, Sadie listened intently as Robb filled her in about
the latest social events or offered his opinions about politics and
economics. Eventually her mind would drift back to Irene, however,
and she would ask about new developments in the treatment of
tuberculosis. The doctor did his best to offer optimism where there
was none.

The budding friendship between Mrs. Cody and Dr. Robb did not go
unnoticed in the community. It was well known that the doctor was
already keeping company with another woman, a local schoolteacher.
Sadie herself was aware of it and asked others about the relationship.
When they described it as presumably platonic—"Robb is just toting
her around"—Sadie was clearly pleased. Her efforts at appearing
nonchalant backfired, however. Her friends were attuned to her
interest in Robb and knew about his long visits at the mansion. The
resulting social buzz was all about the doctor and the *widow*, not the
schoolteacher.

Sadie's friends cautioned her about Dr. Robb. He had been in the
area for only a short time and no one really knew much about him,
they cautioned. Sadie countered by stressing how helpful Elmer had
been in offering advice about Irene's treatment.

Her friends were not deterred, however. A few described Robb
unflatteringly as a "ladies' man" who was using the schoolteacher as
"bait" to land the "real catch," the wealthy Widow Cody. Such insinua-
tions disgusted her. People could talk all day about "fishing" but she
had no intention of getting hooked. She was too intelligent to be

susceptible to the charms of a fortune hunter. Besides, her primary interest was in restoring Irene to good health again. What she needed was a friend and a medically knowledgeable confidant, not a new husband.

But the devious Dr. Robb had other plans. In Sadie he saw for himself a future, one he could not easily secure by his own merits. Through his medical experience he had learned how to detect when a patient was depressed, anxious, or fearful, and such a person responded to comfort and reassurance. Sadie Cody fit the description. Robb's visits to the mansion became more frequent, and the heart-to-heart talks grew longer and longer.

Even from Green Bay, Louise Spear was well aware of the budding relationship between Sadie and Robb, and she immediately reacted in a self-righteous manner. She viewed Robb as a charlatan and could not fathom why Sadie was oblivious to his real motives. Her only conclusion was that her friend was falling in love.

The idea that Sadie was courting while Irene lay dying thoroughly disgusted Louise. She reacted not with concern or caring, but with indignation. On her next trip to Sturgeon Bay, she snubbed Sadie and uncharacteristically stayed with Harriet Hart. Louise twisted the dagger by making sure her visit was duly reported in the *Advocate*. As a close friend of both women, Harriet was caught in the middle, like a referee separating two determined prizefighters. Louise was furious at the thought of Robb's nocturnal visits to the mansion, and Sadie was terribly hurt to be abandoned by her longtime friend. The newspaper article made public the painful quarrel. There might as well have been a front-page headline: *Why isn't Louise staying at the mansion with Sadie?*

Harriet did her best to make peace. She contacted Sadie, trying to reassure her that Louise was not meddling so much as just showing concern, though quite clumsily. Sadie was still miffed but, at Harriet's suggestion, she agreed to host a party at the mansion in honor of Louise. Formalities ruled the day. At evening's end Louise politely thanked the host, then retired to Harriet's. The next day she returned to Green Bay, never again to set foot in the Cody mansion. A longtime friendship was irreparably broken.

Furnace Murder

Sadie was deeply saddened by Louise's disloyalty. They had been such dear friends, and she couldn't understand why Louise should be so sanctimonious when it came to Sadie's personal affairs. Harriet Hart spent a week in Green Bay trying to patch things up, to no avail. She returned to confirm the worst—Louise was no longer Sadie's friend. About the same time, the sanatorium notified Sadie that Irene's condition had deteriorated and not much more could be done for her.

On April 16, 1912, the Titanic sank. News of the tragedy shocked the world and dominated even the local newspapers. But Sadie was unmoved. Next to her own misfortunes, the Titanic disaster seemed miniscule.

On May 13 Sadie left to visit Irene for a week. When she returned home, her social calendar was empty, devoid even of the regular card parties. Shortly after Independence Day, Louise Spear made another visit to Sturgeon Bay. This time it was no surprise that she snubbed Sadie.

By August the rift with Louise hardly mattered to Sadie. She spent another week with Irene at the sanatorium. Just four days after returning to Sturgeon Bay, she was called back to Stevens Point, with news that Irene was in critical condition. Harriet Hart accompanied Sadie, and the two stayed a week before returning home. A week later a telegram arrived, urging Sadie to rush back to the sanatorium due to Irene's deteriorating condition. She felt like a ping-pong ball but nonetheless she sped to her daughter's bedside.

The next evening, August 23, Irene Cody died. She was only twenty-three years old. When Sadie returned to Sturgeon Bay, she brought home the body of her daughter. Four years earlier, Richard Cody "lay in state" at the mansion. Now it was Irene's turn.

Three days later the funeral was held at the mansion. The *Democrat* reported that "Irene Cody was mourned by a very large circle of friends. She was a popular and brilliant student who was interested in all the better activities of school life." Friends and relatives from all around the state attended. Conspicuously absent was Louise Spear.

~ ~ ~

Rowe and Dodd

Alone in the mansion, Sadie Cody reflected sadly on the past year. She had tried in vain to save Irene, just as she had tried with her mother and Richard. She had expeditiously responded to every call of distress, had always been there when her daughter needed her the most. Even at the end, it seemed Irene had waited for her mother to arrive before dying. During the last weeks, the two had ample time to share time and private thoughts. Both knew the gravity of the situation, and both had come to accept the sad reality that Irene would never leave the sanatorium alive.

Sadie was now alone in the world. No one was left of the Marsh family, no living relatives at all except for a few distant members of Richard's family. Mother, Richard, Irene—each of their deaths had devastated Sadie. Death was natural, she reminded herself, as she recalled the words of her minister at the successive funerals. There was nothing natural about betrayal, however, and the enormity of her bitterness toward Louise Spear dwarfed even her sadness.

8

Doctor in the House

In deference to her daughter during the four years between Richard's death and Irene's, Sadie Cody had not broached the subject of remarriage. Clearly Irene would have opposed the idea—she had repeatedly warned her mother about fortune seekers, just as trusted advisors had. Yet in those lonely days while Irene was dying at the sanatorium, Sadie did not see anything wrong with periodical visits with Elmer Robb. The two were being discreet about it, she felt. Her friends disagreed.

For more than a year Robb resisted making overt advances on Sadie, as she struggled with the seemingly inevitable death of her only child. But he made a practice of visiting the mansion on those cold winter evenings. He readily gave advice to allay the fears and frustrations that were consuming Sadie and shared his medical expertise relating to tuberculosis. Though Robb felt he too was being discreet in his visits with Sadie, yet town gossips saw through his "discretion." The doctor and widow's budding romance was the talk of the town, and judgmental critics blamed Robb for the tragic breakdown in her long friendship with Louise Spear.

From the moment Robb moved to town, he had watched with hypnotic fascination the comings and goings of Sadie Cody and marveled at her elaborate mansion, the showplace of the community. How much was she really worth? He was not alone in his inquisitiveness—the extent of her wealth had tantalized curious town residents for years. Everyone knew she was wealthy. Just *how* wealthy, no one new.

Robb was not in the same league as Sadie, financially or socially, and he knew it. His medical practice earned him less than $600 a year, a respectable amount but nothing that gave claim to affluence. Then there was his daughter Ladye, who compared very poorly to Sadie's daughter. Irene had been a refined and educated young woman, whereas Layde was unsophisticated, even crude. Robb himself was forced to admit that the name "Ladye" clashed with his daughter's unladylike demeanor.

Much of what he did during his early days in Sturgeon Bay appeared to be calculated. He moved to an upscale neighborhood, only a couple of blocks from the town's grandest mansion. Next he hosted his own "coming out party," featuring his daughter Ladye as hostess. To be sure, he had on hand Miss Chandler, his schoolteacher "friend," to minimize any faux pas that Ladye might commit in front of the sixteen, socially elite attendees.

Robb dreamed of becoming the most highly esteemed doctor in town. More practically, though, he strived to marry Sturgeon Bay's wealthiest woman and lord over her vast financial domain. It was a stretch, he knew, but he even tried to visualize Ladye as part of a happy, new family. Dreaming was easy but making it all happen was a challenge.

Robb had appealed to Sadie's vulnerabilities, her loneliness and fear that her only daughter lay dying. His medical knowledge certainly had been useful in that respect—probably his greatest asset. His initial attempts to establish himself in the community had nearly been sabotaged by the outrageous Louise Spear, but in the end he won out. Louise's desertion of Sadie only worked to his advantage. But daughter Ladye was proving to be a real liability, and Sadie showed little interest in developing a rapport with the uncouth young woman.

Robb forged on. Irene's body was barely cold when he appeared at Sadie's door for a heart-to-heart talk. He had anticipated this moment for months and was well prepared. There they sat in the lonely mansion, surrounded by the remnants of Sadie's happier past. Once again his unctuous condolences were graciously offered and accepted. He worked hard to show Sadie how much they had in common. She had lost a husband—he, a wife. He too was lonely. He too needed companionship. He too desired a respectful standing in the community, not the shallow pity extended disingenuously to widows and widowers.

He also honed in on Sadie's greatest regret: Richard's death could have been prevented had she sought out a knowledgeable specialist. Over and over she lamented, *Why weren't there specialized doctors in Sturgeon Bay?* This same scarcity of specialists had also meant taking dear Irene to the sanitarium in Stevens Point, 150 miles away. And for what? To die. He could become that specialist, Robb insisted to Sadie, but he could not do it without her support. Perhaps he wanted Sadie to think he needed her emotional support, but clearly it was her financial backing that he coveted.

Robb even played the "Irene card." "Your daughter would want you to move on and be happy, not to dwell on death," he argued. "You are educated and sophisticated, and I am a professional man. We can move forward together, we'll make a beautiful couple. Surely Irene would approve wholeheartedly."

He had more ammunition. He could assist with the many financial problems she would face and protect her interests. In return she could help him continue his education and specialize in the treatment of eye, ear, and throat ailments. Yes, he would have to be away months at a time to complete his training, but when he returned to Sturgeon Bay, he would be a specialist and Sadie could be a specialist's wife. Besides, he remembered to add, he loved her.

From afar it may have appeared to be a cockamamie scheme, but it worked. On September 28, 1912, Sadie Marsh Cody became one of the few persons of her time to enter into a pre-nuptial agreement with a future husband. The agreement read:

> Mrs. S.E. Cody hereby agrees to appoint E.H. Robb general manager of her property with the exclusive agency of property to the amount of $6000, all for a period of four and one half years from date – to not sign any contract invalidating her estate or sell real estate without his knowledge and approval – to settle up the estate under the will, discharging the present executors or administrators and thus acquire an unrestricted control over the estate. Also to loan $5000 additional upon signing this contract – $500 on or about Feb. 1st, 1913,

and the remainder as needed for financing his business all on his note of hand and not to exceed seven per cent interest.

E.H. Robb agrees to fit himself for the practice of the specialty of eye and ear – to give his care and attention to the management of the estate and upon the fulfillment of the above agreement, to marry and provide for the said S.E. Cody, the mutual intention being for the marriage to take place during the month of February 1913.

So much for Robb's protecting Sadie's interests! Nonetheless, the agreement was signed by both parties. Irene had been dead less than five weeks.

A few days later Dr. Robb left town to pursue his post-graduate studies in Chicago. As reported in a local paper, he had been "preparing himself for some time for the specialty of eye, ear, nose and throat." He returned to Sturgeon Bay to visit Sadie for a few days in mid-November and again near the end of December.

On New Year's Day 1913, Elmer Robb and Sadie Cody were married in a "quiet ceremony" at a private home in Oshkosh, Sadie's hometown. In happier times Sadie had reveled in the holidays—they were of almost mystical significance to her. But those wonderful times with Richard and Irene were gone forever. Marrying on New Year's Day was symbolic, signifying hope for a brighter future.

Despite the rumors in Sturgeon Bay about the impending marriage, many locals were caught off guard when it took place. The *Advocate* reported, "The little affair was quite a surprise to friends of the couple, who were not let in on the secret as to when the interesting event was to take place." *Interesting event*—an unusual term for a marriage.

Immediately following the ceremony, Elmer and Sadie honeymooned in Chicago, where he managed to complete his medical studies. Meanwhile, Ladye Robb headed back to Newton, Iowa, with intentions of becoming a nurse. The daughter was gone and that was fine with Sadie—there was no room at the mansion for *that* lady.

Furnace Murder

The newlyweds returned in mid-January to take up residence at the mansion. Robb, now a specialist, needed a more spacious and elaborate office, and within weeks relocated to an ideal location downtown. Sadie again became socially active in church and civic affairs and attended meetings of the Woman's Club. Robb made the most of his new social status by joining the Knights of Pythias, an organization in which Richard Cody had been a leader. And his professional advertisements in the local newspaper continued to appear in almost exactly the location where Richard had advertised.

During the first months of the marriage, Sadie's friends began to notice her becoming less vivacious and more withdrawn, even morose. The weekend visits to friends in other cities that characterized her previous life were now conspicuously absent. Many speculated that Sadie, despite her new life with Robb, was still grieving for Irene. Others suspected that all was not well in the marriage.

What was *really* happening in the confines of the magnificent mansion? Few knew. Sadie cloaked her personal matters in the same secrecy as she did her personal wealth. To most, however, it was obvious that Robb wanted even more than medicine as his profession and the mansion as his residence. He seemed to have a voracious appetite for money.

He wanted to control it all. Unsatisfied by the powers he had attained under the pre-nuptial agreement, he pressed for more and more control over her property and financial holdings. At first Sadie reluctantly agreed to shift some power, but soon he was conducting financial transactions without her authorization, often even without her knowledge. When she learned that her new husband was wheeling and dealing behind her back, Sadie consulted her advisors behind *his* back. This infuriated Robb and led to bitter quarrels.

Despite growing evidence, Sadie could not bring herself to believe that her husband was only out for her money. She still wanted the love and companionship he had promised. Publicly she made every effort to project the appearance that all was well at home. Maintaining the status in the community she had while married to R.P. Cody was very important. The last thing she wanted was to become a laughingstock.

Rowe and Dodd

By September Louise Spear had heard of Sadie's recent troubles and planned a visit to Sturgeon Bay for a firsthand view. Sadie heard about Louise's impending arrival, so she parried it by heading off with Robb for a concurrent three-day visit to Green Bay, Louise's hometown! Those who followed the social pages in the local papers found it all intriguing and delightful.

It was no laughing matter for Sadie Cody, however. She realized she had already conceded far too much power to her greedy new husband and that her stature in the community had plummeted. What she feared most, though, was that Robb might be planning to sell her entire estate without her knowledge or consent. Making matters even worse was the growing realization that Louise Spear had been right all along.

9

Denouement and Divorce

How quickly the honeymoon was over! Sadie Cody's life with Robb was rapidly deteriorating, and she was mortified by it all. But just when she so desperately needed the support of her friends, she cut way back on her social activities, ceasing entirely to host even her popular card parties. And she was too embarrassed to face the advisors who had been forewarned her about Robb.

The prenuptial agreement had been bad enough, but Sadie particularly regretted her decision, signed in writing just a week before the wedding, to give Robb power of attorney over her vast holdings. Now he was holding all the cards and was ready to deal. No longer was he kind, sweet suitor who wooed her. Now he made demand after demand, and if she hesitated he would become enraged and threatening. Sometimes he'd take off for days, leaving her to wonder where he was and what he was doing. Typically she was the last to learn that he was sleeping at his downtown office, eating at a local hotel, and telling anyone who would listen how difficult it was to live with his unreasonable wife.

It was a very public war, and a legal one as well. On April 9, 1913, just three months after his wedding, Robb filed the power of attorney document and a similar agreement with the county Register of Deeds. Both instruments were in effect for four and one-half years. The maneuver gave Robb full control over all of Sadie's finances and holdings, except for her beloved mansion, which she steadfastly refused to cede to him.

By 1914 Sadie was fighting vigorously to prevent Robb from plundering her estate. But he fought back, becoming more demanding and often violent. He thrust yet another document at her, this one requiring her to pay him $300 if she "interfered" with his management of her estate. Sadie still thought her marriage could be salvaged, so she broke down and signed.

The feuding continued. The more power she relinquished to him, the more he wanted. Their bitter quarrels typically occurred in the privacy of the mansion, where he made wild threats: He could accuse her publicly of lying, of "being insane." As a physician he could easily have her committed to an asylum. He would consume her estate, Sadie feared. So she signed yet another agreement, giving her husband even more power and agreeing to pay him $2000 if she interfered or revoked the agreement. Another pitiful mistake, she knew, but it was a desperate, final attempt to save her marriage and reputation.

Predictably nothing changed. In fact, Robb grew even more contemptuous of her and outrageous in his demands. It was time to face reality, Sadie knew, but she feared he would stop at nothing. He was fully capable of evicting her from her beloved mansion and institutionalizing her.

With little left to lose, Sadie finally stood up to him. In May 1915, Robb left the mansion for an extended period, and on July 25 Sadie revoked all his powers of attorney. A week later Robb filed for divorce. He realized he had pushed her too hard and lost control, but illogically he believed that a divorce action would bring her to her knees. When it didn't, he quickly withdrew it.

The Christmas season of 1915 would be another lonely one for Sadie. Two days after Christmas, Robb again filed for divorce but once again dropped it when Sadie refused to yield to his threats. She had reached her limit. Probably she had already lost most of her vast wealth to him—there was no way of knowing for sure—and her public image was in shambles. What he was doing to her was nothing short of blackmail. There was no turning back, it was time to retaliate—time for Sadie to administer to Dr. Robb a taste of his own medicine.

On December 16, 1915, Sadie Cody served legal papers on Elmer Robb, charging him with illegally using her money to purchase a mare and colt valued at about $225 and transferring ownership of the animals to his sister Mary Robb. Though it was the mansion that was truly at stake, it was two horses that finally brought the warring couple to trial.

Sadie's attorney and trusted friend, William E. Wagener, questioned Robb during a discovery hearing. His goal was to penetrate the tangled financial web the doctor had woven in converting Sadie's vast wealth to himself and his sister. Robb was under oath, but would he be truthful?

> Wagener (Q): Have you any real estate in your own name?
> Robb (A): I have not.
> Q: Have you any money on deposit in any bank?
> A: I have not.
> Q: Have you any money put away any other place?
> A: I have no money, except a small amount in my pocket.
> Q: Is anyone holding any money for you?
> A: No.
> Q: You credited yourself June 14, 1915, with $2300. What has become of the money?
> A: It has been spent.

Frustrated, Wagener continued trying to expose Robb's stash.

> Q: You credited yourself with $4532 on the Anderson mortgage. Where is that money?
> A: It has been expended.
> Q: Can you name the items the money was expended for?
> A: I couldn't give an itemized account of it.
> Q: How long has it been since you had anything to do with the Cody estate?
> A: Since last August.

Conspicuously absent was any mention of the mare and the colt. Wagener bore on, attempting to force Robb to explain his claims against his wife.

> Q: You have charged $2300 in damages against Mrs. Robb *for interfering with her own business?*

A: Yes, sir.

Q: How much of Mrs. Cody's property do you claim to be
  your own?

A: $6423.

Q: But you've already taken $2300 for liquefied damages, is
  that correct?

A: Yes. She still owes me $4123.

Wagener had exact amounts, but he was determined to pin down
Robb on his devious expenditures. Exasperated, he pushed on.

Q: *What has become of all the money, doctor?*

A: It has been expended.

Q: What is your yearly income from your profession?

A: About $600 last year.

Q: You drew on April 5, 1915, a check for $2355.73 from
  your joint account with your wife. What was done with
  that?

A: I transferred it to my personal account.

Q: In addition to all this money, Mrs. Robb let you have
  $5000 *more?*

A: I borrowed $5000.

Q: You never repaid it?

A: I performed services for Mrs. Robb and had claims
  against her.

Q: Did Mrs. Robb know how you were using her accounts?

A: She pledged not to look over the accounts or to interfere.

Without any mention whatsoever of the mare and colt, the discovery
proceeding drew to a close. Robb's self-serving answers had been
incriminating, yet the overriding question of what had happened to
Sadie's money had not been answered. Robb's own attorney must have
been pleased—he offered nary a single objection to Wagener's questions. So where was the money? The deafening answer was— *gone.*

The actual trial for the theft of horses was heard by a circuit court
jury in March 1916. Sadie lost. The jury found on behalf of Robb's
sister and ruled that Sadie had "unjustly detained" the two animals on
her livestock farm in Jacksonport. It was in the awarding damages,

however, that the jury spoke most loudly: Mary Robb was awarded only six cents! Sadie gladly paid—to expose Robb and his sister as fools was well worth the pennies.

Sadie was now on the offensive, and in August 1916 *she* filed for divorce. Then she reconsidered and withdrew the action. The days dragged on and Sadie's loneliness intensified. Finally, in the silence of that great house, stark reality hit her. Despite public humiliation, despite everything she had endured, it was time to rid herself completely of Robb.

She telephoned her attorney and told him she wanted the divorce and this time would not be backing down. On November 8, the papers were filed. Notably, the plaintive signed as "Sadie E. Cody." As a legal precaution her attorney appended the name "Robb." Sadie wanted no part of Elmer Robb, or his name, ever again.

The divorce case languished in court proceedings for almost a year, but when it was finally heard in September 1917, it became a real media event for the small city of Sturgeon Bay. In fact, it was the front page story on two of the three local newspapers. For three-and-a-half days, everything was aired in a courtroom crammed with town gossips eager for all the messy details. The court found on her behalf:

> Robb used persuasion, threats, humiliation, and publicity of their domestic troubles . . . to prevail upon the plaintiff to execute new agreements and take control of large sums and shares of the plaintiff's property. The defendant has no love for the plaintiff and caused her great worry and concern . . . and treated her in a cruel and scornful manner and charged her with being insane and called her vile names. On one occasion he used force and violence to eject her from his office.

The court found that Robb had embezzled nearly $10,000 from Sadie, a staggering amount in those days. The money, for the most part, was gone. Sadie was awarded alimony of $15 per month to be paid from the doctor's estimated annual earnings of $780. At the conclusion the judge granted Sadie's most salient request—restoring the name she proudly used before her disastrous second marriage, "Sadie Cody." On

Rowe and Dodd

November 8, 1917, exactly one year after she had officially filed for divorce, Sadie was freed forever from the clutches of Elmer Robb.

The long ordeal was over but it had left her a broken woman, publicly disgraced and the butt of cruel jokes. The once proud mistress of the manor retreated into the great house. Distraught, she faced yet another Christmas filled with hopelessness and despair.

The divorce also ruined Robb. It crushed his aspirations, smeared his personal and professional reputation, and all but destroyed his medical practice. He continued to run professional advertisements for about a year but then left town for what was called an "extended visit to Chicago and cities in the East." Only once more did Robb surface in Sturgeon Bay.

~ ~ ~

Once again Sadie Cody was alone in the world. The period following Richard's death had been excruciatingly painful, but now things were even worse. She desperately needed someone who would listen, a trusted friend to whom she could share her tortured thoughts and feelings. But there was no one.

Impelling questions haunted her: Why had her entire life fallen apart just when the magnificent mansion reached completion? When she and Richard were attaining the pinnacle of success? Why had God destroyed her?

Her social status demolished, she had become an object of derision. Following the public airing of her messy divorce, many people gleefully speculated that her once vast fortune was mostly gone. She thought back to the sinking of the Titanic in 1912, how the tragedy barely phased her because it coincided with the final months of Irene's decline.

Now it was 1918 and the news of the day was the sinking of the Tuscania, a troop ship torpedoed by a German submarine off the coast of Ireland. Down with the ship went 2000 American soldiers. Most survived but 210 did not make it, including two young soldiers from Sturgeon Bay. Sadie envisioned herself on that doomed vessel—would she have been among the ninety percent who survived or the ten percent who didn't? She would have gone down with the ship, she guessed.

Two years later Sadie Cody's regrettable history with men was reprised. Fortune hunters were still staking her out, and her life would take yet another bizarre twist. In September 1920, Sadie visited relatives in Oshkosh, where she had wed Robb eight years earlier. She was ready to marry for the third time and wanted to test their reactions. Predictably the relatives disapproved and strongly advised her against entering another relationship that could end in a fiasco. Sadie didn't like their verdict so she sought out a new panel of judges, traveling to Marinette to visit Richard's relatives. They were less disapproving, so it was their advice that she followed.

On December 4, 1920, Sadie married a traveling salesman, C.J. Kersten. They were wed by—of all persons—the same reverend who married Sadie and Robb. The long fingers of the *Door County Advocate* latched on to the story: "The bride is most favorably known in our city where she has resided for many years. Mr. Kersten is a popular traveling salesman." Her friends reacted negatively. Marrying a traveling salesman was, they felt, an act of desperation designed to drown out her continuing sorrow and loneliness.

Elmer Robb heard the news but did not send the newlyweds his congratulations. A month later, he appeared in Sturgeon Bay for the last time. His purpose was to file a petition to free him from making further alimony payments to Sadie. The court granted his request.

C.J. Kersten and Sadie Cody—it's not clear whether she ever adopted her new husband's last name—spent the Christmas holidays not in the mansion but in Milwaukee. Shortly thereafter the marriage collapsed amid wild rumors that Sadie tossed Kersten from the mansion, screaming after him that he was nothing but a "cheap fortune hunter." The marriage was over and Kersten soon left Sturgeon Bay. No record of a divorce is known to exist.

It was yet another humiliating experience for Sadie, and she became even more reclusive. She cut off nearly every social tie except activities at Hope Church and the Woman's Club. But despite the loss of her former lifestyle, Sadie remained her feisty self when it came to finances. Even after Robb's looting, she still had money to loan! In 1926 she loaned $2500 to Wisconsin Fruit Farms at a rate of six percent interest. Ten years later the note still had not been paid, so Sadie sued and was awarded full principal and interest.

By 1936 Sadie had few friends left, though she still maintained some contacts. For example, Sadie was invited to serve as hostess at the wedding reception of the daughter of Sturgeon Bay's longtime fire chief. One attendee remembered her fondly as a "tiny lady who seemed to delight in participating in the event."

To many town residents Mrs. Cody represented a fascinating contradiction of elegant pride and pitiful financial collapse. A local merchant, then just a little boy, recently remembered how she'd once come into a paint store and haggled over the price of paint even while wearing fancy white gloves—with holes in the fingers! And she had been proudly wearing the elegant mink coat that Richard had given her decades before.

~ ~ ~

In 1939 Louise Spear died at age eighty-five in Green Bay, having lapsed into senility. Sadie Cody did not attend the funeral. The one-time fast friends had been dead to each other for twenty-seven years.

Sadie would outlive Louise by nine years though, like her former friend, she too would die at the age of eighty-five. Her remaining years were laden with the same sadness and despair that characterized the decades following daughter Irene's death in 1912. In her waning years Mrs. Cody was described by some as kind and well-intentioned, while others were far less charitable. In the end, though, she would be remembered neither by her grand life before Richard's death nor by her pitiful social decline in the years afterward. Instead it would be her dreadful demise that would forever be linked to her name.

Part III

10

Enter William Drews

The fates of Sadie Cody, Sheriff Hallie Rowe, and even young Harvey Rowe would be unwittingly changed by the actions of an unassuming, middle-aged man named William (Bill) Drews. Bill was a reasonably social person who was liked by many acquaintances yet really understood by no one, perhaps not even his closest family members.

Born in 1897, Bill was raised along with two brothers and a sister on a farm near Wittenberg, Wisconsin. His father was described as a "farmer in poor circumstances." It is likely that Bill and his brothers became farmhands at an early age, and this would explain the end of schooling for Bill at age fourteen. After obtaining his eighth-grade diploma from a rural school, he headed straight back to the farm, where he stayed until the age of thirty-one.

Drews married Margaret Long in 1929, and two years later their daughter Audrey was born. In 1933, son Roger was born, but he died four months later from "convulsions." Undoubtedly the death of their infant son took a heavy toll on Bill and Margaret. Finally in 1940, Patsy, their last child, was born.

Bill has been described by family members as a friendly, outgoing "people" person who loved music, dancing, and playing the accordion. Bill's daughters, still living, describe their childhood family as close and loving. There were lots of great times, such as when their father played music and taught the girls how to dance.

Bill was a hard worker but his vocational history, like that of many of his generation, was defined by a brutal economic recession followed closely by World War II. In 1942, Bill moved his family to Sturgeon Bay, where he joined the war effort by building warships in the local shipyards. When the war ended, so did his job. Bill soon found a job with a local oil company. He drove a gas and oil truck, making home and business deliveries to customers all over Door County. Whenever he could, he took young Patsy along for the ride.

The year of 1946 would be an especially cruel one for the Drews family. Bill began seeing Julia Smith, who was divorced with four children. He sometimes described Julia to others as a "family friend." The problem was that he never told his family about her and she was undoubtedly more than a mere friend. The affair was not entirely secret, though, and it must have been very painful to Margaret and bewildering to Audrey and Patsy.

On March 19, 1946, Bill and Margaret were on their way to a dance that they were going to attend with close friends. There was a one-car accident and their vehicle became engulfed in flames. Margaret perished in the inferno, while Bill walked away with non-life-threatening injuries. It was the end of the Drews family as they had known it. Audrey remained with her father to continue at the local high school, but young Patsy was sent to live with relatives three hours away.

Two years later Bill Drews and Julia Smith were living in separate apartments in the same building and were ready for marriage. But he had recently lost his job at the oil company and was becoming financially desperate. The only person he knew who had money to spare was his landlord, Sadie Cody.

11

Murder: Day One

Friday April 2, 1948

At 7:00 a.m. the great bells of nearby St. Joseph's Catholic Church rang, awakening Sadie Cody for what would be the last time. Spry for her age, she launched into the day. Her first task, as always, was to carefully straighten the sheets and quilt on the little cot in what used to be the day room. Now it was her "bedroom." Many years ago it had been her husband's law library, and the shelves were still crammed with his books of law and business. It was odd, she knew, but spending most of her day, and night, in the room seemed to bring Richard back into her presence.

She donned her favorite pair of slippers, ancient though they were, and peeked in the mirror. Her reflection was the same as the day before. *Thank goodness!* she thought, considering her age. In the kitchen she lit the stove to heat some water that she would use to wash up in the bathroom. She had neither city water—turned off years before to cut expenses—nor a water heater. She didn't mind improvising in this manner—there was plenty of time to wait for the water to warm. Being frugal felt good.

She went from the kitchen to the sitting room at the front of the mansion, where she picked up a pair of little binoculars. From one window to another she went, trying to get the best view of the neighborhood. To the north she looked directly into the living room of her neighbors. She wished the Rowes still lived there instead of the renters—there were too many comings and goings and she couldn't even be sure who all were living there. The Rowes had been so quiet and predictable that they weren't so interesting to watch, but that never stopped her from spying. She liked them. Sheriff and his wife got along well, and their son was never any trouble at all.

She switched windows and leveled her binoculars at the Burkes' house across the street. It was too early for any activity on the large, enclosed front porch. Nighttime, though, was a different story. Loretta was a night owl and Sadie could always count on her sitting on the porch in the dark, her matches flickering and cigarettes glowing. Spying on each other—it was a game they played, surreptitiously trying to get the one-up on each other's activities.

Up the street a little way were the VanDreeses. In a half hour Peggy would be making her way over to the schoolhouse where she taught sixth grade, while her husband would head out to work at the drugstore. She wasn't entirely sure what Allie McLaughlin's morning routine was, because she couldn't see her house, two down on the same side of the street. Allie was such a good friend, and talkative! Sadie could count on finding out all the happenings during their daily afternoon chats.

By now the water on the stove was warm and it was time to wash up for the day. Laid out in the bathroom from the night before were a fresh towel and new bar of soap, niceties that complemented the ornate, marble washbasin. She had nearly forgotten that she would need to fix herself up a little nicer for the afternoon meeting of the Woman's Club. It was about the only organization she still belonged to, and today high school students would be presenting a musical and a dance recital. She really looked forward to it.

As she made her way into the kitchen through the formal dining room, she checked one more item—the little chip of wood on the bell box above the telephone. It was her unique way of detecting when she'd missed a call while away from home or in part of the house where she couldn't hear the ring. The vibration of the bell dislodged the chip, causing it to fall to the floor. "Chip on floor" meant missed call. It was a very clever device, if she said so herself! This morning the chip was intact—no one had called.

In the kitchen she removed from the cupboard the same arrangement of utensils as always: one plate, one cup with saucer, and one setting of silverware. Now she was ready for her breakfast of tea and toast. The menu rarely changed, though sometimes she splurged by topping her toast with a spoon of orange marmalade. Just another ordinary meal, taken in her lonely house, isolated from the world. She hated self-pity, so she forced her thoughts onto other matters of the day—reconciling the rents from the tenants of her properties and preparing for the afternoon meeting of the Club.

Like breakfast, morning chores followed a deadly routine. Dusting was one. It always had to be done, though she rarely had visitors and no one would know the difference. Then she would head back to the kitchen to wash, dry, and shelve the breakfast dishes she'd left soaking. Next she would review her account logs to make sure every bill had been paid and to note which ones were coming up in the next week. It was more of a ritual than necessity, as her mind was sharp and she rarely forgot anything related to finances. Finally she would take a few moments to read the local newspaper. If she stayed on schedule, she would be sitting in front of her big front window just in time to watch the children pass by on their way to school. She watched partly out of simple curiosity and partly for deterrence—maybe her presence at the window would discourage young vandals from breaking off more boards from her decaying, front-yard fence.

Watching the lively children helped ward off a painful image that frequently invaded her memory—young Irene heading out the front door and off to school. For distraction she forced herself to recall how young Harvey Rowe used to go by on his way to school, before his family moved to the jail. As he walked along her fence, he'd lightly tap the top of each slat, as though counting them. Finding a wobbly one, he'd bend over and try to push the loose nail in with his thumb. She never had to worry about *that* boy. He was a friend, and a protector of her fence.

After all the schoolchildren had finally passed by, Sadie moved from the window and placed her hand on the back of her favorite ornate chair. Then she stared at the old piano, another grand reminder of the past—it hadn't been played in years. Sitting quietly with Richard, listening as young Irene played for them, was . . . . It was another image she had to force from her mind.

Rowe and Dodd

Next she sat down at her card table and began reviewing the rent receipts from the tenants in her two rental houses—one on the east side of town and a better one on the west side. Luckily, most of her tenants paid on time. Occasionally one or another was late by a day or two. It was Bill Drews, on the east side, who was usually several days behind. As of this morning, he was one day late.

She put on her reading glasses and turned to the newspaper—the breakfast dishes could wait. As always, she first scoured the obituaries to see if any of her old friends and acquaintances had passed. And to make sure her *own* name didn't appear—an old joke, of course, but at eighty-five she allowed herself to indulge. Next she turned to the hospital admissions. Two weeks ago an acquaintance had been admitted to the hospital, and the following week she made the obituaries. Sadie often wondered how she herself would die, crossed her fingers and hoped the end would be quick and painless. She recalled how Louise Spear had died slowly of senility.

Below the hospital admissions something caught her eye: "Licensed to wed, Wm. Drews and Julia Smith at Green Bay, April 3." Grabbing her pencil she made a checkmark next to the announcement. How interesting! Both were her tenants in the east side house. Although they lived in separate apartments, it seemed suddenly clear they had been "shacking" together. Bill was unemployed and Julia herself was occasionally late with the rent. Now they were getting married— how could they even pay for a wedding ceremony? And what about afterwards—would they move into one apartment, creating a vacancy for her to worry about, or take off and leave her with two unrented spots?

This was a marriage that wasn't good for business. She would have to make it clear to Bill when he came to pay his rent that she would not tolerate any such arrangement. They would have to pay both rents until she was able to find a new tenant for the unoccupied apartment. She would be very firm with Drews. All of it was very upsetting.

To calm herself, she focused on her usual late-morning trip to downtown. *Did she have anything to mail?* Her first stop was always the post office, where she picked up her mail, hoping for something

80

personal but rarely finding it. Then she'd go to the grocery, where she could expect to be treated rudely. *Remember to take the milk bottle for return.* Her last stop would be the bank, the one where her husband had been president. Back then she had been treated like a celebrity, now she was just another customer. She brought out her purse and, before putting it on the table near the front door, double-checked that it contained the $110 in rent money for deposit.

~ ~ ~

At 10:25 a.m. Bill Drews walked out the front door of his apartment building and pulled hard on the knob. The door didn't latch so he gave it an extra pull. He would have to complain to old lady Cody about it, not that she would have it fixed. He strolled to his car at the curb and climbed in. Instinctively he turned to check the floor of the backseat. It was silly being so suspicious—who would want to hide in *his* rundown car? If he were so afraid of an intruder, why not just lock the car doors at night? Unwilling to do that, why fear trouble?

He proceeded toward his destination seven blocks west. He could be walking—the exercise might do him good. But there was a reason he rarely walked anywhere. People would immediately assume his car was out of commission, that he didn't have the dough to keep it running. What people think about my car is more important than what they think about my waistline. The thought made him chuckle.

Three minutes later he pulled to the curb just past the corner of Fifth and Louisiana, turned the car off, and sat for a moment to collect his thoughts. His pitch to Mrs. Cody would have to be perfect for her to open her pockets—she was a tough nut to crack. Calm enough now, he checked his hair in the rear view mirror. Then he got out of the car, crossed the street, and approached the mansion.

He climbed the porch steps and rang the doorbell. It was broken. The old lady wouldn't even repair her *own* doorbell, so he knew it was futile to ask her to spend a few bucks to have his apartment door fixed. He knocked on the heavy door and grimaced as his knuckles barked a little. His arthritis was getting worse. When she didn't open the door right away, he made a fist and pounded three times.

Rowe and Dodd

The door cracked open and he noticed her beady eyes peering out at him through the narrow space protected by the door chain. What was she so worried about? Who would rob an old lady in broad daylight?

She closed the door, removed the chain lock, and reopened the door to the uninvited guest. He knew she would, since he owed her rent. "Mr. Drews," she announced needlessly. He said nothing, simply following her into the living room, or the *sitting room*—whatever a dame like her might call it. But she didn't invite him to sit. She just stood there, waiting, he supposed, for him to fork over the rent.

The time had come. Drews had thought about it in advance. She was old and alone, probably a real creature of habit. Probably went downtown every day to shop, or to the bank to check her balance. Rent was due yesterday, so she'd have a small bundle from all her renters who paid on time. But somewhere in the gaudy mansion, there might be a stash of hundreds of dollars, maybe thousands. Plenty to meet his loan request, or at least pay for a wedding and celebration afterwards.

"I won't be needing the apartment any longer," he began.

"I know," she replied, surprising him. "I read about your marriage plans in the paper. Let me tell you, if you're planning to move in with Mrs. Smith, or the both of you are going to move out on me, you're going to have to pay. At least until I get someone to replace you. Remember the thirty-day notice clause, and that goes for both of you."

Earlier that morning Drews had imagined telling her about his upcoming wedding, and in his mind Mrs. Cody had offered him warm congratulations, not heaped abuse upon him. The lady had a one-track mind—money! He had to get back to the plan, calm things down before he popped the big question.

"As you know, I'm out of work right now, and I've got the wedding to pay for. So I don't have the April rent." He paused, gauging her reaction. She glowered at him.

"But I'm working real hard to turn the corner. To support my new wife and her family and, of course, my own two girls." He searched the lady's face for a hint of kindness, but there was none. "I've got a real estate deal going. It's almost final, except I need $2000 for the down payment." Again, Mrs. Cody made no response. "I'm going to buy land and go into farming. I know I can make it work. It'll take a little time but I'll be able to pay off everything. Can you lend me $2000? I'll pay any interest rate you want."

Now the lady reacted. "Ha! You're no farmer, Mr. Drews! If I lent you that money, it would be the worst investment I ever made."

He bristled at both the insult and the refusal. He wasn't willing to beg but he did lower his sights. "Mrs. Cody, we've known each other for a long time. I've never given you any trouble and you know I do my best to pay you on time." He paused, hoping the old lady would soften a little, but she just continued to glare.

"Can you at least lend me a little for my wedding? Just a couple of hundred, maybe three hundred, would be great. Even without the farm, I've got a line on another job and you know I'll be good for it."

"Get out! You'll be hearing from my attorney. And go ask Mrs. Smith if she's afraid of becoming your wife. Afraid of going up in flames, like your first wife!"

Her remark infuriated him. Ever since his wife Margaret had died in the car accident two years ago, he had heard the whispered accusations and had tried to ignore them. Finally he had reached his limit. He slugged Mrs. Cody hard on the left side of her head. She crumpled to the floor. He looked down at her lying at his feet and saw blood trickling from her nose, then noticed his right hand still in a hard fist. She moaned a little but seemed unconscious. Where was her purse? He could take the rent money and get out of there. With a little luck, he'd get his $200. With a little more luck, he'd be long gone when she snapped to, and she wouldn't remember a thing.

But what if she came out of it and remembered everything? She was a friend of Sheriff Rowe's, and she would phone him right away. A posse would be on his trail in minutes. He had to act quickly. He bent over and carefully picked the old lady up, cradling her in his arms. She weighed practically nothing, probably less than his little daughter! What to do with her?

He headed into the hallway and quickly found the doorway to the cellar. He started down the steps and immediately became aware of how narrow the stairway was, and how dark it seemed. He knew he should look for a light switch but decided just to take his chances. Turning sideways he negotiated his way down the stairs. Suddenly the old lady shifted in his arms and he jerked reflexively, badly scraping his right hand on the rough stone wall. Instead of pain he felt an overwhelming rage come over him. Finally he reached the bottom of the stairs. Daylight was streaming in through the half-windows. He blinked as his eyes tried to adjust.

There was the furnace directly in front of him. With barely a thought, he opened the door and stuffed her into the firepot, face-first. After manipulating her spindly legs through the small opening, he slammed the door tight. For the first time he looked at his throbbing hand and could see blood seeping from the wound. He was sweating profusely, his head pounding out two questions—*How can I cover up my crime?* and *How can I stop my hand from bleeding?*

The first problem seemed easy to address. He reached for the stoker switch, turned it, and heard the furnace roar in response. To be sure he opened the draft, feeding in more oxygen. Then he looked around and spotted a cistern, removed its lid, and peered in. Luckily it was full of water, so he dunked his bleeding hand into the tank and felt immediate relief.

As he ascended the cellar stairs, he tried to convince himself that his plan would work. People might assume that Mrs. Cody was out of town visiting friends for a few days. When she failed to return, they might figure she had been kidnapped. But who would want to kidnap an old lady? The cops around town aren't exactly the smartest bananas in the bunch—they might spend months trying to solve her disappearance. Who would suspect Bill Drews?

As he emerged from the stairway, he was blinded by the sunlight streaming into the mansion. There must be a bathroom nearby, he thought, and it took him only seconds to find it. He examined his hand more closely and was glad he had only a bad scrape, not a deep cut. At the sink he opened the water faucet but there was no water. Next he tried the bathtub faucet, again without luck. *Damn that cheap old lady. She's had her city water turned off!*

Blood was now dripping from his hand all around the bathroom. He had to stem the bleeding. At first he considered using one of Mrs.

Cody's nice towels but decided against it—too incriminating. Instead he grabbed an old rag that was hanging nearby and wrapped it around his hand.

She must have a purse full of dough, he reminded himself. He recalled seeing her purse near the front door, and when he reentered the sitting room he immediately located it on a card table. He tore it open and discovered good luck for the first time since entering the mansion—the rent money! He took the neat stack of bills from the envelope and, without counting it, shoved it into his jacket pocket. But he wanted more than a couple hundred dollars.

He was beginning to panic. How long had he been in the mansion? Taking a deep breath he reminded himself to stay calm. Though searching the entire three-story mansion for hidden loot might prove to be a wild goose chase, he could at least give it his level best.

He spotted Mrs. Cody's little nightcap sitting neatly on the pillow of her daybed. He picked it up and began using it as a fingerprint eraser, as he searched every place he could imagine for her stash. From drawer to drawer and cabinet to cabinet he went, constantly wiping surfaces as he went. He found nothing. His only remaining option was to head upstairs, but that seemed far too risky. He had never set foot up there and didn't know the territory. Plus, what if a nosy neighbor knocked at the front door or even let herself in—had Mrs. Cody locked it after inviting him in? He could be trapped upstairs without an escape route. And maybe there was no hidden loot.

Back to the bathroom to cleanup. With the old rag, now bloodied from his hand, he tried to wipe up the blood drops from the sink and floor. It was an impossible task, he just kept smearing it all. Finally he "threw in the towel," or rather, tossed the bloodstained rag into the bathtub. Hopefully the bumbling cops would assume the old lady had cut herself cleaning.

With the nightcap still in hand, he hurried back to the cellar to check the situation in the furnace. He swung open the firepot door and could see raging flames consuming the frail old lady. Soon nothing would be left. *Should he burn down the entire mansion?* He quickly dismissed the idea—things were too busy around the neighborhood, too many potential witnesses. Plus, the fire department was only two blocks away, and after the fire was doused someone might find the partially consumed body in the furnace. Better to let nature take its course. Eventually, all the coal would burn away, taking with it all evidence of the body. And with no body, there could be no murder, right?

He was starting to panic again—time was running out! He dropped the nightcap near the furnace, shot up the cellar stairs, and looked around. How long had he been in the mansion? Checking his watch he realized nearly thirty minutes had already passed. It was time to get out, and the backdoor was his best escape route.

As he stepped outside, he breathed a huge sigh of relief. Making his way down the narrow driveway that separated the mansion from the small house next door, he seemed to remember that the Rowes had lived there before Hallie was elected sheriff. He tried to walk slowly and calmly, as if he had just finished a service call. Reaching the front sidewalk, he casually walked across the street to his car and took one last look around. To the best of his knowledge, no one had even noticed him.

Bill Drews sensed that he had just committed the perfect crime, but just in case, he needed an alibi. Julia, his bride-to-be, would want to know how he hurt his hand, and others might inquire as well. He put the car in gear and pulled out into the street, driving directly past the mansion. Glancing at his watch he noted it was 11:05 a.m. With two quick right turns, he headed for Kellstrom's service station on Fourth Avenue. There he told the attendant he'd been having trouble with his back tire, it kept going flat. The attendant dutifully removed and inspected the tire but could find nothing wrong, so he put it back on the car. Flush with money now, Drews pulled out cash to pay not for a repair or a new tire, but for an alibi.

Next Drews headed home to see Julia, who immediately noticed his hand and asked what had happened. "Oh, I had a flat tire and the tire iron slipped." She gently cleaned and bandaged the wound for him.

At 1:00 p.m. Bill and Julia headed for Green Bay, forty-three miles away. Everything was falling in place. Back at the mansion Mrs. Cody was slowly disappearing from the face of the earth, the roaring furnace would take care of that. Now he and his fiancée could begin their new life together. With the old lady's money in his pocket, they went on a shopping spree.

12

Murder: Days Two and Three

Saturday, April 3, 1948

It was just another Saturday for the residents of Sturgeon Bay. Some awoke, perhaps to the bells of the Angelus, while others stayed in bed a little longer. The city itself seemed to rise slowly to life, spring just around the corner. School kids, glad for the weekend, began to appear in front yards just as adults in cars headed into the downtown area.

The afternoon before, a nauseating odor slowly began to invade the area, and it still lingered. A few residents of the neighborhood began to realize the stench was strongest near the Cody mansion. Speculation was that a squirrel must have fallen down the furnace chimney, perhaps burning alive. One passerby remarked, "Old lady Cody must really be stoking up the furnace today. Wonder what she's burning?"

I remember that morning vividly. At the jail two blocks away, my first whiff of the day was of that awful, putrid smell. It was the same odor I smelled the prior afternoon while sitting in my eighth-grade classroom. My mind—like that of any fourteen-year-old boy's— grabbed the most macabre explanation: *It's the smell of burning flesh!* But when I saw Dad following his normal Saturday routine, unconcerned, I pushed the thought out of my mind. He once told me about finding the body of an old lady who had been incinerated in a cabin fire. If anyone would know the smell of burning flesh, it was Dad.

Still, I was concerned so I hopped on my bike and went exploring. The odor seemed to be everywhere but I couldn't locate its source. My best guess was that someone was burning an animal corpse, maybe a raccoon or possum.

At the rental house where William Drews and Julia Smith maintained separate apartments, the two were preparing for the most festive of occasions—their wedding. But Bill's hand was still hurting. Even though they had applied bandages and ointment the day before, not only was the hand not healing, it was festering. He thought of the old lady—had Mrs. Cody burned up completely? How long until she would be missed? Were authorities even now trying to locate her? He reassured himself that the local police were too dumb ever to link him to her disappearance. There was no motive or signs of a struggle, and no one had seen him at the mansion, he assumed.

Besides, he had played his cards right by enriching his alibi: Who could possibly commit such a heinous crime in the morning, go on a shopping spree that same afternoon, *and* get married the very next day? It didn't stand to reason. He knew he had committed a horrific crime, but rationalized that it had been an accident, a knee-jerk reaction to the old lady's cruel remark about the death of his first wife. Nevertheless, even Julia might turn on him if he were linked to Mrs. Cody's death. It would never happen, though, because no one would ever discover the body. The idea of murder would remain a mere rumor, a theory. He had not committed the "perfect" crime, because he'd left the mansion with only $110 instead of the hundreds or thousands he'd hoped for. Still, he was home free.

Julia was calling to him, "Have you made sure that Ed and Helen are ready?" They were to be the witnesses at their marriage ceremony scheduled to take place that afternoon in Green Bay. The two couples were soon on their way. As he drove, Bill thought of the day ahead. Their trip would be a quick one. At the Brown County Courthouse, a judge would perform the brief ceremony, pronouncing him and Julia "man and wife." The real fun would come later.

After the ceremony, the couples enjoyed a quick lunch before heading straight back to Sturgeon Bay for a night of celebration. They hit one bar after another before settling in at Bill's favorite, the Greystone Castle on the west side of town. There they partied well into the night. Bill was jubilant and bought rounds for everyone. No one knew at the time that it was Sadie Cody who was paying for it all.

~ ~ ~

Sunday, April 4, 1948

It was not until Sunday that the ghastly, bizarre story of the murder of Sadie Cody began to unfold. As usual, scores of persons passed the mansion on their way to the several churches in the neighborhood, one of which was Hope Congregational, Mrs. Cody's church. She was so regular in her habits, always making the short stroll at the same time every Sunday morning, that neighbors could set their clocks by her. This morning, as Loretta Burke monitored the action from the porch of her home directly across from the mansion, she found it odd that Sadie was late. Perhaps I missed her, Loretta thought, so with particular vigilance she watched for her old friend to return home after service. It did not happen.

Loretta was Sadie Cody's closest friend in those years. I know because I never heard anyone else, even my parents, call Mrs. Cody "Sadie" to her face. Several times a week Sadie would drop in to visit with Loretta, and the two would enjoy rolls or cake.

To Loretta, Sadie's absence was terribly worrisome. She hadn't seen or heard a word from her friend since Wednesday evening, when the two ladies walked together to visit a friend a block away. Perhaps she had seen her briefly on Thursday—Loretta couldn't remember for sure. If Sadie had been planning to leave town for a day or two, she would have let Loretta know. Something was wrong.

She tried phoning Sadie throughout the day, to no avail. Darkness was falling and Loretta began to panic. Why wasn't Sadie answering her phone? Where *was* she?

Three weeks later Mrs. Burke would be testifying in court.

District Attorney: What happened Sunday evening?

Rowe and Dodd

Loretta Burke: I got nervous. I was alone, and one of my neighbors wanted me to go to a show, and I said, 'No, I'm expecting a call from my husband.' And I called Sadie to come and sit with me and I tried from 7:00 to 8:00 to get her but she didn't answer, so I got alarmed and I said, 'Operator, put a good ring on that line; I can't get her.' So she did but there still was no answer, and I said, 'Gee, it's funny I can't get Mrs. Cody. I haven't seen her for a couple of days.' The operator said, 'Why don't you go and see?' And I said, 'Gee, I don't like to go alone.'

So I sat down and waited for a light to go on, but it never did. Then I called Alice McLaughlin and said, 'Have you seen Sadie?' She said, 'No,' so I said, 'Something must have happened to her. She has fallen down or something.' And she said, 'Let's go and see.' And I said, 'We don't want to go alone.' She said, 'I'll call a cop.' And I said, 'You come over and call.'"

It was shortly thereafter that Allie arrived at Loretta's door and was ushered into the house. Allie placed the call to city police, and two officers responded, including one who was extremely tall and well-built. "Boy, was I glad to have that big cop with me in case anything happened," Allie later told me. It was in the dark of night, and Mrs. Burke brought a flashlight, as did the two officers.

The foursome walked across Church Street and up the steps onto the large front porch of the mansion. Mrs. Cody had entrusted Loretta with the location of a hidden key, so she retrieved it and soon all four were standing inside the front door.

District Attorney: Will you describe for the jury what you saw when you got in there?

Alice McLaughlin: It looked as if somebody had walked out the door, left everything behind. But there was a thick layer of dust on the floor, and I know Mrs. Cody would never tolerate that. It struck me that all the doors between rooms were open, but she always kept them closed."

Furnace Murder

The "dust" seen by Mrs. McLaughlin, it was later determined, had come from the furnace. Fine sediment from the remains of Mrs. Cody's charred body had flowed from the furnace up the cellar stairs and settled throughout the house. As the four walked through the first floor of the mansion, they had no idea they were actually trampling on Sadie's remains.

> District Attorney: Tell us what you saw when you went into the house.
>
> Loretta Burke: We couldn't find any lights. We turned the switches on but there weren't any bulbs in the lights. But I had my flashlight, so did the officers. We looked around and thought we would find her lying at the foot of the stairs or on the floor, because she climbed on things quite high. We looked around the first floor and didn't find anything. The officers went upstairs but I said, 'I'm not going to climb stairs because it is hard for me,' so I stood at the foot of the stairs. When they came down, we all went to the cellar door. Mrs. McLaughlin and I stood at the top of the stairs while the two policemen went down. One of them yelled up, 'Well the fire is out and the stoker is running so I'll shut it off.' I said, 'All right, you shut it off and I tell her when she comes home.'

Next one of the officers took the witness stand.

> District Attorney (Q): Now officer, what did you see or find or observe in the house that evening?
>
> Officer Joseph Antonissen (A): As soon as we got in, I noticed a peculiar smell in the house, and we walked into the living room, into the library and through the bathroom and into the kitchen and everything seemed to be in order. We went upstairs, looked around and came back down. Then we went into the basement and you could smell it worse. You could also smell a hot electric motor.

91

The stoker was running and it felt very hot, so I shut it
off.

Q: Were there electric lights on?

A: The only light we got was in the living room. We couldn't
find switches anywhere else in the house, and if there
were switches there were no bulbs.

Q: You did everything by flashlight?

A: Yes.

Q: You opened the furnace door?

A: Yes.

After finding "everything in order," the officers ascended the cellar
stairs and the whole group exited the mansion. On the front porch the
two officers and the two ladies spoke for several minutes in hushed
tones before going their separate ways.

In her concluding testimony Loretta Burke summed up her feelings about that evening: "After I returned home from searching the
mansion, I sat up until midnight, just praying that Sadie would come
home. Or that I would see a light come on, maybe we missed her
somehow. Finally I went to bed but I couldn't sleep, thinking of what
could have happened to her."

The court transcripts do not adequately describe the eerie state of
the magnificent old mansion on that night—the light switches that did
not work, the ghastly odor, and most of all, the mysterious disappearance of the little old lady.

One of Mrs. Cody's secrets had been exposed. For years she had
gone virtually without lights. As bulbs burned out they were not
replaced, nor were the switches that wore out. Like the four sleuths
who searched for her, Mrs. Cody herself routinely found her way
around the mansion with a flashlight—she always kept one nearby.
Investigators would later find her favorite flashlight on the card table
in the living room, next to the empty milk bottle she planned to return
to the store that fateful Friday morning. Her beloved mink coat was
still draped over the back of a chair.

13

Murder: Day Four

Monday, April 5, 1948

At 7:30 a.m. Mom was at the bottom of the stairs in the sheriff's quarters, "rousting me out" as she always put it. "Time to get going!" I rolled out of bed, ready but not entirely willing to pursue another day in eighth grade.

In a jiffy Mom was serving breakfast in the jail kitchen. By that time Dad had already left for the post office. He always had a post office box, even when he was Conservation Warden. That way he got his mail first thing without having to wait for mail delivery later in the day. Unlike me, Dad was a go-getter.

Shortly after 8:00 a.m. he arrived back at the jail and announced, "I just saw Allie McLaughlin at the post office and she asked me to come over to Mrs. Cody's house to look around. She thinks something may have happened." He told how Allie and Loretta Burke and two officers went through the house the night before and found nothing.

Mom asked him a few questions about it, none of which Dad could answer. But Allie was our friend and former neighbor—she'd requested his help so he was going to give it to her. "As soon as I look through the mail, I'm going over to the mansion and get to the bottom of this." Soon he was gone, eagerly heading out for an exciting morning just as I was reluctantly moseying along for a boring one at school.

Moments later Sheriff Rowe drove up to the Cody mansion in his unmarked car. Allie McLaughlin was waiting for him on the front sidewalk, and Loretta Burke called out from across the street, asking

93

them to wait for her. Allie again filled the sheriff in on their experiences from the previous evening. Up onto the large front porch they went. After Loretta once again removed the key from its hidden hook and opened the door, they entered. The stench immediately hit the sheriff with full force. Instinctively he recognized the odor but pushed away the image of burning flesh. He had other possibilities to explore.

He knew of Mrs. Cody's penchant for climbing up on chairs or footstools to clean, so he guessed she had gone to the attic and accidentally fallen into the cistern. Armed with his favorite high-powered flashlight, Sheriff told the women, "I'm going to start in the attic and work my way down, covering the entire house. Stay here till I get back."

In the third-floor attic, Sheriff found a couple of old large trunks. One by one, he slowly opened each trunk lid and peeked in, dreading the sight of Mrs. Cody's frail body. Then he dragged one of the trunks to the cistern, climbed up, removed the cover, and, after hesitating, peered inside. He was relieved to find no body. His search of the attic had revealed nothing. Next Sheriff moved down to the spacious second floor, where he methodically searched all five bedrooms, looking under beds and in closets. Nothing.

Finally Sheriff returned to the first floor and told the two women he'd found nothing. "Let's look around the first floor again." But everything appeared in order. In the front room, draped over a chair, was Mrs. Cody's fur coat, and on a nearby table sat her purse and an empty milk bottle. All was set for her morning trip downtown—one she never made.

From there the search party moved to the day room, where everything was tidy, her bed made. Then the bathroom: "Ladies, don't touch anything. It looks like we have blood on the wash basin and some spots there in the bathtub." His theory was still that she might have hurt herself, and the blood fit. "I'm going downstairs," he said. "Maybe she's in the basement, injured." This time the two women followed their leader down the narrow cellar stairs.

Sheriff did a quick survey of the large cellar. It was filled with old furniture and stored boxes but, not surprisingly, it did not seem cluttered. *Mrs. Cody sure is tidy,* he thought. He noticed a small cistern next to the stone wall. Slowly he lifted the lid, just as he had done with the larger cistern in the attic. Half expecting to find a floating body, he found nothing but water.

The sheriff now turned his attention to the furnace and noticed an old-fashioned nightcap lying on the floor nearby. It seemed odd that Mrs. Cody would have carelessly left her cap on the floor. Checking all around the furnace, he saw nothing. Sheriff's thinking was now shifting: Maybe she had been taken from her home by force—abducted. But that awful odor was strongest in the cellar. A light bulb lit in his mind, and he took a long, hard look at the furnace.

Sheriff opened the firepot door, switched his flashlight on, and peeked in. There was no flame—it was dark as death inside. First he shined his flashlight on the ashes and charred bits of coal, then poked his entire head through the opening. That's when he spotted it—a human skull, completely white, with no signs of hair or skin! Prodding it with his flashlight, he detected what appeared to be remnants of brain. He also found two elongated bones.

Sheriff Rowe no longer had a missing person's case on his hands. This was murder! His mind was racing, even as his head was still in the furnace. He remembered his two fellow sleuths—Mrs. Cody's closest friends—and he knew that they deserved to be the first to know. While still inside the stove, he considered how to convey the terrible truth. Finally he withdrew from the firepot, his face was glistening with sweat though the furnace was stone cold. "We don't have to look any further for Mrs. Cody. Someone killed that poor old lady and burned her to death, and she's in this furnace." Both women gasped and Allie broke into tears.

The women's emotional outburst upset the sheriff. As the authority figure, he knew he had to stay collected, in control. To buy himself a brief moment, he turned slowly back to the furnace and glanced in again before slowly closing the fire door. He was not a funeral home director, he was the county's chief law enforcement officer. It was not his responsibility to console the bereaved—he had a murder investigation on his hands. He led the ladies back upstairs, where he picked up the telephone and called the city police. Romy Londo, my favorite cop, answered. Sheriff said, "Romy, I'm at the Cody house. Get the chief and tell him to get up here, and I want you too. We've got ourselves a murder." Romy, who never walked anywhere, responded, "I'm temporarily without a squad car." Realizing it was futile to try to persuade the officer to walk even two blocks, the sheriff said, "Wait there, I'll pick you up!"

As required by law, Sheriff called the coroner. Now he had to decide what to do with Allie and Loretta. He couldn't just turn them loose and risk the news spreading like wildfire, but he didn't have time to debrief them before leaving to pick up Londo. He instructed the two women to lock the door behind him and stay in the house until he returned. "Don't touch *anything*, and don't allow anyone to enter."

Within minutes Sheriff returned with the coroner and Romy. Now he took the time to properly thank the two women and make them swear not to spread any information whatsoever. Then he dismissed them. It was an awkward moment. Allie and Loretta had been lifelong friends of Sadie's, and it had been *their* persistence that led to the horrid discovery of Mrs. Cody. But now they were civilians and probable witnesses at trial, so they needed to leave the crime scene.

Police Chief Frank Parkman soon arrived, followed shortly thereafter by District Attorney Ed Minor. It was becoming quite a gathering, so Sheriff told Parkman he wanted the premises secured. An officer was immediately stationed in the front yard to keep unauthorized persons, especially curiosity seekers, away from the premises.

Dad arrived home at noon, just as I showed up for lunch. Together we headed toward the kitchen—I couldn't wait to see what Mom had whooped up for lunch. Up until then, it was just another mundane Monday for me, and probably for Mom too. Then Dad spilled the beans. His words were so traumatic I'll never forget them. Almost with indignation he asked, rhetorically, "Well, you want to know what happened to Mrs. Cody?" We both nodded silently. "Someone murdered that poor old lady and burned her up in the furnace."

Mom and I were stunned, and for a moment we stood in silent disbelief. His words seemed to hang suspended in the air, as we slowly began to consider the gruesome situation. Finally Mom asked, "What are you going to do, Hallie?" He replied, "We're meeting at one o'clock at City Hall. Ed Minor wants to call in help from outside."

~ ~ ~

Although it all happened decades ago, I remember it like yesterday. None of us, including Dad, was really prepared for everything that would follow. In a matter of an hour or two, the entire community of Sturgeon Bay would be engulfed in a wave of fear. But our first thoughts were only of poor old Mrs. Cody, our dear former neighbor. It was as if we had lost a close relative, not to natural death but to unspeakable violence.

Mom and I both knew Dad had to detach himself from his personal feelings in order to do his job. That's why, I suppose, neither of us cried that day at the lunch table. How could we? As a family it was our responsibility to be strong and to support Sheriff in whatever needed to be done. Of utmost importance was that the crime was solved quickly and the murderer brought to justice. I know Dad accepted the challenge as his professional responsibility, but he must have felt the need for personal revenge as well.

Murder was not something that happened in my hometown. Sure, there had been killings in Door County over the years, but nothing that attracted national attention. No one was prepared for the scores of reporters and photographers from around the country that descended upon us. Though I would see her photo and read her name in the newspaper for weeks to come, I never could fathom that the victim really was Mrs. Cody, the sweet old lady who had been our neighbor, gave me Christmas gifts, and welcomed me in to visit when I brought over the cake and cookies from Mom.

I was a great lover of horror movies, but what I was watching on the screen of life was almost too much for me. The killing was so macabre, the victim so real—how I wished it were a dream, or a picture show that I could just walk away from at the conclusion.

~ ~ ~

After the noon hour—and the worst lunch of my life—I returned to school, my heart heavy and my mind weighted down by the news. I was in no shape to concentrate on my teachers' lesson plans. Instead I dreamed of being next to Dad in the thick of the investigation.

Ed Minor was waiting at City Hall for the arrival of those he considered to be his "underlings." Having previously served as city attorney in Milwaukee County, Minor considered himself to be a "big city guy," and he was already ranting about this case being too big for the local cops to handle. "We need professional help on this!" he exclaimed, not realizing how offensive his remarks were to Sheriff Rowe.

After conferring only briefly with the sheriff and others, Minor called his friend from Milwaukee, Dr. Samuel Pessin, a pathologist. Pessin dropped all of his other important duties and headed straight for Sturgeon Bay. Minor also summoned Charles Wilson, dubbed the "crime doctor," who had just been appointed the first director of the new State Crime Laboratory at Madison. Meanwhile, Dad had already called a local pathologist to determine if the bloodstains found in the bathroom were indeed human blood. They were.

There was no radio station in town, but that didn't stop the news from spreading like wildfire. Telephone lines were tied up throughout the county. Husbands called home, ordering wives to take the kids inside and lock the doors. The local hardware stores were soon sold out of padlocks and guns. It was mass hysteria, and this was *before* word leaked out to the national press! Within hours reporters from all the major wire services, plus the Chicago and Milwaukee daily newspapers, were on their way to little Sturgeon Bay.

The *Green Bay Press-Gazette* reported, "After thirty years of virtually no violent crime, local residents are shocked and baffled by a major murder mystery that rivals anything they have ever heard or read about." The next morning, the *Milwaukee Journal* quoted District Attorney Minor as saying, "There's no question in my mind that this is a murder." The *Chicago Sun-Times* picked up on the quote: "Minor says it's a clear case of murder." The *Milwaukee Sentinel* called it "one of Wisconsin's deepest murder mysteries," and also quoted Minor as saying, "it is unquestionably murder."

Furnace Murder

The district attorney was puffed up about all of the quotes, but his statement was inane—*no one* was contending that Mrs. Cody crawled into the furnace on her own! Even young children appreciated how ludicrous the statement was. For years thereafter, whenever people discussed the mansion murder, Ed Minor's silly remark was gleefully repeated.

Finally Wisconsin Crime Director Charlie Wilson arrived at the scene. This was his first big case, his initial opportunity to show what he could do, how brilliant he was. Wilson was all too happy to reconstruct the crime scene for a reporter from the *Chicago Sun-Times*, "It happened sometime Thursday night, after Mrs. Cody, thrice married, carried in the evening newspaper from the porch. She probably was stabbed in her bedroom off the parlor, where bloodstains were found on the floor."

The only thing wrong with Wilson's analysis of the crime scene was—*everything!* He got every single detail wrong, including the date, time of day, location and cause of death, and blood on the floor. What the "crime doctor" would be best remembered for, though, was his exhaustive but futile search for fingerprints over the next several days. He dusted the mansion thoroughly, and when he could not lift a single print, he dusted some more. His failure was spectacular and led inevitably to jokes that he needed to go back to fingerprint school! Wilson would later testify that the reason he found no fingerprints was because the shrewd killer had diligently wiped the whole house clean. Unfortunately Wilson's explanation was belied by the fact that the killer failed even to clean up his own blood in the bathroom.

At 8:30 p.m. pathologist Samuel Pessin finally arrived at the scene and began the grisly task of methodically removing each of Mrs. Cody's bones from the furnace's firepot. The setting was like a Hollywood drama. The cast consisted of Pessin and two assistants, plus a handful of police officials, and the entire scene was illuminated by high-powered lights. On the floor was a diagram of a human figure that had been meticulously drawn to represent a tiny, eighty-five-year-old lady. Carefully Pessin removed bone after bone from the furnace and placed them on the diagram, leaving no doubt that the bones belonged to Mrs. Cody. The location of the bones in the firepot, and even their order of removal, revealed how she had been shoved into the furnace. The only question remaining, and it was searing everyone's mind, was: *Had Mrs. Cody been burned alive?*

At midnight the gruesome task was completed, floodlights extinguished. The last remains of Sadie Cody, along with the old-fashioned corset she had been wearing, were finally laid to rest on the cold floor of the cellar. Dr. Pessin testified at trial that the order of the bone removal indicated the victim had been shoved into the firepot headfirst. The position of her hands and arms near the skull led to the even more horrific conclusion that Mrs. Cody had tried to protect her face from the raging flames. She *had* been burned alive!

Even though it was a school night, Mom let me stay up waiting for Dad to get home. She knew I wouldn't be able to sleep. A little after midnight, in walked Dad. He was exhausted and wanted to go straight to bed, but Mom and I stopped him in his tracks. We wanted every last detail. It took nearly an hour, but finally we heard it all. Never before—at least never in school—had I listened so attentively. Everything was branded into my brain. I couldn't wait to get to school next day to tell everyone, but Dad made me swear to keep my mouth shut.

~ ~ ~

The mansion stood in eerie darkness. Once a grand symbol of wealth and prosperity, now it represented the pall of fear that blanketed our city. Under Sheriff Rowe's orders the mansion had been sealed off and armed officers stationed to protect the crime scene.

The excitement at the mansion was not over, however. Deputy Jack Pivonka, one of those assigned to keep watch, reported the following morning that someone had attempted to enter the house in the middle of the night. But no one had been apprehended and no one else had seen anything, so Pivonka's claim was widely disregarded, even by Sheriff.

Four decades later I learned what actually had happened that night when a local man finally let the cat out of the bag. Several teenagers had drawn straws to determine which one would try to sneak into the mansion for a good look at the crime scene. The one who drew the short straw crawled over the backyard fence and approached the north side of the Cody mansion, where he tried to enter through an unlocked basement window.

This was his chance! Just as he was crawling through the window, a hand came from nowhere and grabbed his shoulder. He ran like hell, and when he got back to his buddies, he excitedly claimed that the ghost of Mrs. Cody had grabbed onto him and tried to pull him into the furnace. As the youngsters grew to adulthood, they often reminisced about the prank and continually accused "Short Straw" of lying about the hand on his shoulder. But there *had* been a hand that night—Jack's! Officer Pivonka *had* told the truth. That might have been the only time Dad was ever wrong.

14

Murder: Day Five

Tuesday, April 6, 1948

By Tuesday morning the serene little city of Sturgeon Bay had been transformed into a community paralyzed with fear. How could someone enter the most famous home in town, brutally kill a defenseless little old lady, and then depart, completely undetected? Things like this did not happen in small towns. Residents feared for their lives, and doors that had gone unlocked for years were now tightly secured. And there was little confidence that small-town law enforcement could solve the case.

Sturgeon Bay was getting nationwide attention for the first time. Crime reporters from all around the Midwest descended upon on the city, like vultures hungry for a lead that would give them an exclusive story. Photographers swarmed the whole area from downtown to the mansion.

Where was I? In school—*very* reluctantly, believe me. I looked out from the windows of my eighth-grade homeroom constantly to see what was happening at the mansion only a block away. I was sure the reporters would want to interview me and that my picture would be snapped for the papers, if only I weren't incarcerated in school.

The metro newspapers made the murder their lead story that morning. The *Milwaukee Sentinel* blared: "BONES IN MANSION FURNACE; RICH STATE WIDOW MISSING"; the *Chicago Tribune:* "RICH WIDOW SLAIN, BURNED"; and the *Chicago Daily News:* "SLAIN WIDOW IN FURNACE. Mansion Yields Vague Clues."

At noon I sprinted the half block home to learn of the latest events. Lunch was ready, both for the prisoners and for Dad and me.

102

Furnace Murder

Mom seemed proud to have put together such a good meal despite the repeated interruptions and telephone calls throughout the morning.

Mom wanted to know what Dad knew. He just shook his head. "No one saw a thing, no clue why she was killed. I talked with everyone in the neighborhood. No eyewitnesses, no idea of a motive, no evidence of a struggle, nothing." You could tell Dad was really at a loss.

Mom had an idea. "You know, something tells me you should check the renters. Check Mrs. Cody's *renters.*" Dad looked up from his plate, expressionless. He stared at her for several moments, like he was trying to decide whether she was crazy or on to something. Finally he spoke. "Do you know who one of the renters is?"

"No," Mom answered.

"You remember about two years ago, the guy whose wife burned to death in the car on Bay Shore Drive?" Yes, she remembered. "Well, that's one of the renters—Bill Drews."

"That's your man, Hallie. This time you have to do something about it, you can't let this go." *This time.* To me that meant there had been a last time.

Dad nodded in agreement. "There's no doubt in my mind he did it, but I have to be able to prove it. And if anyone gets wind of it, we're going to lose him, he'll get away with it."

Turning to me, he said, "Now when you get back to school, Harvey, you never heard the name 'William Drews.' If anyone asks, including a cop, you don't know a thing. Don't mention that name to anyone. I want you to promise me that, because if word ever gets to him we'll never find out he murdered Mrs. Cody." I promised.

Dad knew what he had to do and when it had to be done—now! Only we three Rowes knew who killed Mrs. Cody, and that's the way it would remain, until Dad decided otherwise. As I left for school, I knew my role, small but significant, was to keep my mouth shut.

When I returned to school after lunch, my classmates mobbed me. "Who killed Mrs. Cody?" "Who's the suspect? "Tell us what's going on!" Dad had anticipated it all—how did he know eighth graders so well? He knew I would be tempted to spill my guts, to become the momentary hero. Had it not been for Dad's stern admonition, I would have succumbed and sold out the sheriff for a moment of glory. But now I played ignorant, and if Dad knew how hard that was for me, he would have been proud.

"They don't tell me nothing!" I spat out. "Nobody's got a clue and even if they did, I'd be the last to know." After checking to make sure some teacher wasn't snooping around, I added, for emphasis, "Damn it!" With all my feigned outrage at being left out of the loop, I was putting on a terrific performance. But I worried I was overacting.

I had played dumb to my classmates, and for the rest of the afternoon, I'm sure I appeared plenty dumb to my teachers as well. All I could think of was the Cody case—the lurid crime scene, details of the investigation, and suspicions about William Drews.

When school was finally over, I rushed home to find Mom sitting in Dad's chair in the jail office. Questions were written all over my face, I didn't even have to speak. Mom replied, "I haven't heard a thing, Harvey. Practically everyone in town has called, *except* Sheriff. They pretend to be offering support, but they're just pumping for info, if you ask me."

Later I found out what Dad had been up to since lunch, and it was clear he'd had no time to handle courtesy phone calls. First, Dad approached District Attorney Minor and revealed his suspicions about Bill Drews. This time Ed was ready to listen and the two of them headed for Drews's apartment. No one was there.

They returned to the city police station in City Hall to organize the investigation and prepare a room for questioning the suspect. Sheriff then dispatched a county officer to several locations to check for Drews. Meanwhile, Sheriff began his own pursuit of the suspect. At 3:00 p.m. he instructed Deputy Pivonka, "Come with me to pick up a suspect by the name of William Drews." The two headed back to Drews's residence. When they rapped on his door, Julia, the new wife, opened it. This time Drews was there.

Spotting the suspect, Sheriff invited himself in. "Bill, you've probably heard about Mrs. Cody." Drews nodded affirmatively. "The DA would like to ask you a few questions since you are one of her tenants. Would you come down to City Hall with us?" Without hesitation Drews said he would, but first he headed to a closet. Sheriff tensed with apprehension, but Drews merely removed his jacket from a hook and put it on, without event. Seconds later the sheriff and the suspect headed out the front door.

As Drews walked to the squad car, Sheriff noticed the still-festering wound on his right hand. "How'd you hurt your hand, Bill?" The response was immediate and casual: "Oh, I got it chopping wood out back. A chip of wood hit it."

Sheriff let it drop but felt sure he had his man. The deep wound on Drews's hand was exactly what he was looking for, as it explained the bloodstains found in the bathroom at the mansion and on Mrs. Cody's nightcap. Drews's alibi seemed ridiculous.

Sheriff was taking it one step at a time. He had accomplished his initial goal—to get Drews out of the house and away from his wife. Within minutes they arrived at the police station, and Sheriff escorted the suspect in for questioning. "Keep him here until I get back," he directed Chief Parkman.

Then Sheriff set out, working alone and going strictly on gut instinct. That's how he'd always done his best work, even back in his days as game warden. Stealthily he had targeted his prey—the game violator—and ferreted him out in the wilderness, issuing a citation or hauling the perpetrator to jail, as the offense dictated.

This time the stakes were enormous: a conviction of first-degree murder. The Sheriff not only had to act swiftly and decisively but also had to stay within the letter of the law. He swung by the mansion for one more look at the evidence in the bathroom. There he found the crime doctor, Charlie Wilson, who was unbelievably *still* dusting for fingerprints. Then Sheriff headed straight back to Drews's apartment to "chat" with Bill's new wife. Something told him that Julia was not involved in the crime—probably knew nothing about it—but still, she was the weak link.

He rapped on the front door again, just as he had an hour earlier. Again Julia Smith promptly answered, but this time there was no cheeriness.

"Where's Bill?" She was clearly worried about the situation, whatever it might be.

"I just want to ask a few questions, ma'am. Maybe you can clear up a couple of details." She offered him a seat and there they sat, across from each other, in comfort chairs but hardly comfortable.

Sheriff remembered his manners and congratulated Julia on the wedding. Then he began. "About the money for the wedding. I know Bill's been out of work. Where did he come up with the money, and how much was spent?"

Julia thought for a moment. "He brought $110 home on Friday and we already had $42, so we had enough for the ceremony and a little celebrating."

"How exactly did you spend the money?"

"We went shopping on Friday afternoon. Nothing too extravagant, of course. Bill had gotten his attorney to collect a debt for him and after the legal fee, Bill had $110 left."

"Let's back up a little. When did Bill leave the apartment on Friday morning and what time did he return?"

"I think he left at about 9:30. Maybe it was closer to 10:00. And he didn't get back until about 11:30 or so."

"It took him two hours at the attorney's office?"

"No. After he left the law office he noticed he had a flat tire, so he pulled over and tried to fix it. The jack slipped and he cut his hand, pretty badly. He decided to drive to Kellstrom's and have the guys there fix the tire."

Julia Smith was now suspicious of Sheriff's intent. He hadn't mentioned anything about murder, but everyone in town knew what had happened at the mansion. "Bill had nothing to do with Mrs. Cody's murder, if that's what you're getting at." She reached quickly for a cigarette. She didn't offer the sheriff one.

"Okay, Mrs. Smith. I'm not accusing anyone of anything. What happened after he arrived back at the apartment at 11:30?"

She corrected him, curtly. "It was more like 11:45. We had lunch and left to go shopping at 1:00 p.m. That's it."

Sheriff was experienced enough to know when someone answers "that's it," it usually is. There were more important things to attend to at the moment, so he didn't want to waste time pushing Mrs. Smith further into a corner.

Furnace Murder

"Thank you, Mrs. Smith. Or, I suppose it's Mrs. *Drews* now." The newlywed did not smile. "I appreciate your help and I'll let you get on with your day."

Julia walked him to the front door. As Sheriff thanked her once again and said goodbye, he noticed she was trembling slightly.

Next Sheriff headed straight to Kellstrom's. Bill had lied about the wound on his hand, telling the sheriff one thing and his wife another. Why would he lie about something so insignificant? And what had he told the guys at the service station?

Sheriff pulled into the station and got out of the squad car. A moment later, one of the mechanics emerged from underneath a car, wiping his hands with a shop rag.

"What's up, Sheriff? You hear about Mrs. Cody?" he joked.

Sheriff was in no mood for levity. "Were you working at the station last Friday morning?"

"I always work Fridays."

"Did Bill Drews come in with a tire problem?"

"Sure did and I fixed it, but there wasn't much wrong with it."

"What do you mean?"

"Drews claimed his back tire had gone flat. I took it off and checked for a leak, but couldn't find nothing. So I pumped it up real good and put it back on the car, right rear, I think.

"Did Drews help you with the tire repair?"

"Hell, no. We don't let customers help us."

"Did he have an injured hand when he came in?"

"Yeah, he did."

"Did you ask him how he hurt his hand?"

"None of my business."

"Is it possible Drews tried to change the flat and hurt his hand in the process?"

"Doubt it. The tire was a little low but it sure wasn't flat. And he never took it off the car, if that's what you mean."

Sheriff had all the information he needed, so there was no point in continuing. The last thing he wanted to do, though it was probably too late, was to convey his suspicions to a civilian. He could just imagine the mechanic spreading it all around town that the case was cracked.

Rowe and Dodd

~ ~ ~

Sheriff Rowe had been keeping in touch with the city police throughout the afternoon. "Keep Drews at the station. Just keep questioning him, keep him busy," he told them.

Chief Frank Parkman was trying his best. "Where did you get the money for the wedding and how much was there?"

"It was $110 and I got it wired to me at Western Union by Andy Lowe," Drews responded.

An officer was quickly dispatched to the Western Union office to verify the story. Upon his return a hushed conversation ensued between Parkman and the officer. No such transaction had taken place—Drews had not even been at the Western Union.

Meanwhile, Sheriff knew time was running out. Drews had been questioned intensely now for about three-and-a-half hours by almost every official, including the district attorney. At 6:25 p.m. Sheriff arrived at the station just as DA Minor was emerging from the interrogation room.

Drews had admitted nothing, it had been one lie after another. "Do you want a crack at him, Hallie?" Minor asked. It was a silly question.

Sheriff walked into the interrogation room and took a seat directly across from the suspect, who seemed exceptionally composed for someone who had just been grilled all afternoon. Rowe knew this would be his final chance before he would have to release Drews for lack of evidence.

Three weeks later, Sheriff Rowe's court testimony summarized his questioning of Drews:

> District Attorney Minor: Tell us what happened, what you said to Mr. Drews and what replies he made.
>
> Sheriff Hallie Rowe: I got some paper and a pencil and asked Mr. Drews where he had been and what he had been doing, the approximate time he had been at various places and how much money he spent on his trip to Green Bay. And this was all done in a casual way for about fifty

minutes, possibly an hour. He gave me the same answers each time. I thought we had questioned him long enough in this manner and we might just as well get to the point.

So I said, 'Bill, you know what you are here for, don't you?' He said, 'Yes.' I said, 'Well if you don't know, we want to find out who murdered Mrs. Cody and put her in the furnace and burned her.' I accused him of doing it and he denied it, so I continued to question him very intensely for twenty-five minutes or a half hour, during which time the discrepancies in his statement were pointed out to him. I told him that he was lying, that we had quite a lot of evidence on him, that he might as well admit that he killed Mrs. Cody and burned her.

Dad later told me the vital details of those final minutes, which added considerably to the sterile court record. He had continued to take notes as the suspect answered question after question. He knew Drews was lying, as he had coolly done throughout the lengthy interrogation. But Dad felt that no one had really come down on him hard, no one had actually accused him of the crime.

From all that Sheriff had learned that afternoon and from what he knew of Mrs. Cody's habits, he had mentally reconstructed Drews's actions the day of the murder. Every detail fell into its proper perspective: the milk bottle sitting on the table, waiting to be taken to the store; the dishes that were never put in the cupboard; the blood on the bathtub and sink. Sheriff envisioned Drews appearing unexpectedly at Mrs. Cody's door, asking for money, being refused, and striking out. Injuring his hand somehow during the gruesome murder and trying to clean up in the bathroom.

Suddenly the rest of it came together perfectly for the sheriff. Spurred by the thought of Mrs. Cody's ashes lying cold in the morgue, he was ready to attack her killer. He put down his pad and pencil, looked Drews straight in the eyes, and said, "Damn you, Bill Drews. *You* killed Mrs. Cody, *you* stuffed her in the furnace, *you* burned her to death, and you are not leaving here until you tell the truth!"

Suddenly Drews crushed a half-smoked cigarette and reached for another, but still he denied the charges. Sheriff continued, "Now I'm going to tell you *when* you did it and *how* you did it, then you're going to confess!" When beads of perspiration began to form on Drews's forehead, Sheriff knew he had him. The accusations intensified.

"Bill Drews, you drove to Mrs. Cody's house at 10:30 on Friday morning, you rang the doorbell, and she let you in. You had an argument and you hit her. You carried her down the basement stairs, shoved her in the furnace and killed her. In the process you injured your hand and tried to wash it off in the washbowl. The faucet didn't work so you went to the bathtub, but that faucet didn't work either."

Drews was now visibly shaken, his face ashen as he smoked one cigarette after another. But Sheriff would not let up.

"You killed her for a measly $110. You faked a pitiful alibi to explain your hand, but you couldn't even keep your lie straight. Remember what you told me, and what you told your wife and the grease monkey at Kellstrom's. You've told too many different stories, Bill. You killed that old lady and burned her up!"

Drews sat there, sweat streaming down his face. They know it all, he thought, but how could they? Was there an eyewitness, someone who saw him go to the front door?

Sheriff Rowe was employing a technique that years later would be widely employed by law enforcement to break serial killers. He had switched from asking questions to confronting the suspect with every horrendous detail of the crime, step by step. Drews was shot, his veneer of innocence shattered. He wiped his face and admitted, "Yes, I'll tell. I did it."

Within seconds the small office was filled with the other officers who had unsuccessfully questioned the suspect throughout the afternoon. Ed Minor himself grabbed several pieces of plain bond paper and told William Drews to start dictating a statement. As Drews talked, the DA transcribed.

Three pages later, the confession was complete. After Drews signed it, Sheriff Rowe officially arrested him on a charge of murder in the first degree. Rowe felt like he had invested half a lifetime on the case. When he glanced down at the date on the confession, though—April 6, 1948—he realized Sadie Cody had been dead only four days.

15

Murder: Day Six

Wednesday, April 7, 1948

One day after the arrest of William Drews, Sheriff Rowe swore out a criminal warrant, charging him with the murder of Sadie Cody. It was signed by Judge Grover M. Stapleton. A preliminary hearing was scheduled to determine if there were grounds to hold him for a circuit court trial.

Drews couldn't afford an attorney, so Judge Stapleton appointed him one. The lawyer assigned to represent the highly unpopular defendant was Frank G. Weis, who learned of the order when he returned home from a day of fishing. The historical record does not reveal how many fish he caught that day but, regardless, it was truly an unlucky day for him.

On the day of Drews's hearing, Dad and Mom arose early. Maybe they wanted a little time to themselves, free from my pestering, because I remember they got me up only about two minutes before I was due at school. It's funny, I don't remember getting in trouble for being tardy that morning. Probably the teacher thought I, the sheriff's kid, was a celebrity, just like my pals did.

When Dad picked up the mail that morning, he also picked up Bill Drews's mail that had been delivered to "General Delivery, Sturgeon Bay." In Bill's mail was a copy of the *Milwaukee Sentinel*, with its front-page story headed, "Grudge Motive Seen in Widow's Murder." In the upper corner of the newspaper was the address label that indicated his subscription would expire in June 1948. It would never be renewed.

A later edition of the *Sentinel* had an updated headline: "FURNACE MURDER CONFESSION!" Along with photographs of the grisly crime scene, the story reported how William Drews "broke down after five hours of questioning." Similarly, a headline in the *Chicago Sun-Times* blared: "FURNACE KILLER CONFESSES," and other newspapers ran equally sensational headlines.

While the defendant was being transported to court that day, I was confined to school, though I'd done absolutely nothing wrong! I would have given anything to be in the courtroom gallery, and I'm sure Drews would have given anything to trade places with me in school.

Judge Stapleton presided over the small courtroom in the antiquated old courthouse, and the gallery was jam-packed with spectators eager for fireworks. They were sorely disappointed. In the blink of an eye, Stapleton ruled that sufficient evidence existed to bind William Drews over to circuit court. Then he remanded Drews to the custody of the sheriff, without bail. The dissatisfied crowd slowly drifted out of the courtroom, just minutes after they had rushed in to claim their seats. What a letdown the hearing had been! By contrast, the trial would be spectacular.

I dashed home from school that afternoon. Anyone who watched me sprint past would never have guessed I was the same kid who typically dawdled his way to school every morning. I didn't know what to expect when I rushed into the jail office, but I wasn't disappointed. That morning Dad had received a large cardboard box from Dr. Pessin, the pathologist. He opened it long before I got home and decided its contents were unsuitable for the eyes of his fourteen-year-old son. I protested to Mom, and she took up my case: "Hallie, he's going to see worse in biology lab next year. Anyway, I'm sure nothing can match his imagination."

It was one of the few times I remember Mom prevailing over Dad. Before he let me look inside, he showed me the small index card accompanying the box: "Remains of Sadie Marsh Cody." Then he opened it and removed what was left of the skull, along with a charred chunk of her brain, seared to a crisp. After that came, anticlimactically, several bone parts.

Furnace Murder

For lack of a suitable place, that gruesome box sat on Dad's desk for nearly a week, until funeral arrangements were finally made. Whenever I found myself alone in the jail office, I was drawn to that box. I'd open it and just stare at Mrs. Cody's skull and charred brain. It all seemed so unreal. This was all that was left of the little old lady who had been my friend for about as long as I could remember? I heard her weak voice: *Won't you come in and visit with me for a while?* It was so vivid, it spooked me.

The following day, April 8, the *Door County Advocate* devoted most of its front page to the murder. The headline read: "Confession Follows Speedy Solution to Mrs. Cody's Furnace Murder." The article gave Dad a lot of glory.

> Quiet and unassuming, yet efficient and methodical, Sheriff Hallie Rowe cracked Sturgeon Bay's first murder case Tuesday evening. His logical perseverance of a 'hunch' that deviated from his usually scientific approach led to a full confession by the sinister killer and earned Rowe the admiration of a fear-struck community and fellow officers. Unparalleled in history here, the climax of this almost unbelievable act 'against God and mankind' came just 105 hours after the sadistic crime was committed.

Next to the article was a picture of Mrs. Cody, taken only a few years before. Several times I had asked her to let me take her picture, but she always declined, insisting, "You don't want to take my picture." Once she even told me she thought she looked ugly.

Sometime between her funeral and Bill Drews's trial, the will of Sadie Cody was made public. Everyone was dying to know how much she was worth. Including the mansion, her estate was valued at about $50,000. She left the city $1000 to erect a town clock outside of City Hall. When it came to churches, she played no favorites, leaving $100 each to Hope Congregational—her church—and to the Methodist, Moravian, and Catholic churches of Sturgeon Bay. Another $100 each went to the Sturgeon Bay Library and the Sturgeon Bay Woman's Club, and she also donated generously to veterans' groups.

Rowe and Dodd

I hope everyone who said cruel things about her over the years felt very guilty when they learned of her generosity to her community and her devotion to her faith. After years of vilification, Sadie Cody's true persona emerged following her death—once again she became the grande dame of Sturgeon Bay.

~ ~ ~

Mrs. Cody was buried on April 14, and Mom kindly let me skip school and go to the funeral. Dad served as a pallbearer, and he seemed a little surprised to see me in the audience. Later that afternoon Dad went over to the mansion to check out something for the upcoming trial, and he took me along. The house stood alone, no longer under police guard. We walked up to the front door and Dad produced the once-hidden key, letting us in. Immediately I was hit by the awful smell of death that permeated every nook and cranny. Would it linger forever?

Being in the mansion for the first time since the murder upset me more than anything else, even Drews's lurid confession, the box of human remains, or the funeral. The great house was still beautiful, but it was lifeless—no longer a home. I tried to think about our good conversations and all the times I'd brought cake and cookies to Mrs. Cody, but mostly my thoughts homed in on the cellar and the horrific way she died.

16

The Trial

Tuesday, April 20, 1948

The Cody murder trial would be the most spectacular ever held in Door County. This time I was allowed to stay home from school to observe the happenings. My parents knew better than to send me to school on a day like this—no doubt I'd just make a menace of myself.

Even before the courthouse opened, people lined up at both doors, jostling to claim a coveted seat in the courtroom. Judge Edward S. Duquaine presided, and he limited the number of spectators to three hundred. When the seats were filled the courtroom would be closed. Security was tight.

All of the officers of the court, including Dad, were in the courtroom by 8:00 a.m., long before the starting time of 9:00. William Drews, still in his cell at the jail, awaited the most crucial day of his life. Mom and I were at the jail office, taking seriously our duty of guarding the prisoner until he was escorted to court.

At 8:45 we heard a thud that was so loud it could be heard through the steel walls of the cellblock. Mom shouted, "Something's happening in there! We better go look." We sprang into action, entering the cell area and locking the door behind us to maintain security. We passed through two more steel doors before we arrived at the prisoner's cell, where we found Drews lying on the floor, apparently unconscious.

"Go get your dad, Harvey!" Then Mom realized I couldn't go anywhere without her, because she had the keys. Out of the cellblock we went, relocking the main steel door behind us. By the time we hit the jail office, I was flying and covered the short distance to the courthouse in no time. Funny, I remember thinking at that dire moment how Coach at school never appreciated my athletic skills, so I wished he could witness my cheetah-like speed. I shot through the front door of the courthouse, headed straight to the courtroom, and fought my way through the crowd to Dad, who sat near the front. I whispered in his ear. I can still remember how his head and shoulders drew back in surprise—yet he didn't say a word. Slowly he stood up and the two of us exited as unobtrusively as we could. If spectators noticed, they probably just figured I was being a pest.

Dad fast-walked back to the jail—he wasn't big on exercise and I don't recall ever seeing him run. He hit the jail at full pace and headed straight to the cell corridor, while Mom and I stood guard at the control box. We unlocked the big door and locked it behind Dad after he entered the cellblock. Reaching Drews's cell, he found him on the floor. Dad wanted to get to the apparently unconscious prisoner but the locked cell door separated the two.

There I stood at the controls, my fingers itching to act. Dad yelled, "Open the cell door, Harvey!" Mom countered, "*Don't* open it! He's trying to trick you, Hallie!" Dad repeated, "Open the door! Something's happened to him!" Again Mom intervened, saying "*Don't* open it. Go get help!" Frustrated, Dad was left standing in the cell corridor, inches from Drews, who lay on the floor of his locked cell. Finally Dad realized that arguing with Mom was useless, so he yelled back to me, "Go find Louie and bring him over here right away!" I knew he meant City Officer Louis Jeanquart, also a deputy and trusted friend. So I put my imaginary track shoes on again and took off to find Louie, while Mom remained in charge at the control box.

Court still had not convened as I made my way through the crowd again and headed toward Jeanquart. I whispered, probably far too loudly, "Louie, something's happened to Drews!" Without hesitation Louie sprang into action. As we dashed back to the jail, I did my best to explain the calamity. I must have made some sense, because when we reached home base Louie headed immediately to the cellblock, where Dad was still standing helplessly. The main door to the cellblock banged shut behind him. Mom let me take over the controls—real nice of her—and I released the lever that opened the door to Drews's cell.

As Louie and Dad entered the cell, I remember they were unarmed. It was a cardinal rule Dad strictly enforced—no officer was ever allowed to enter the cellblock with a gun. Drews was a good actor, I suppose, but his feigned unconsciousness didn't fool Dad, thanks to Mom's savvy. The prisoner eventually "came to" and was helped onto his bunk by his captors, who noticed a large gash on his forehead.

Sheriff left Jeanquart in charge of Drews and headed to the jail office, where he placed an urgent call to Doctor Muehlhauser. Fortunately the doctor made house calls and arrived in a jiffy. After a brief examination he applied a pad to the wound, wrapped a bandage completely around the prisoner's head, and pronounced him well enough to attend court. Drews's plot had failed.

By now, several other officers had sensed something was wrong, and they converged on the jail. Sheriff took advantage of the opportunity to give a pep talk: "Now this is it. When we go over to court, he's liable to try anything, even diving through a second-floor window. I want one of you stationed in front of every window and two by each door."

Back in the courtroom, fidgety spectators were wondering what was happening. Sheriff Rowe and most of the court's officers were noticeably missing. Finally a breathless deputy arrived and headed directly to the bench, where he whispered the news to the judge, district attorney, and defense attorney. The courtroom crowd was abuzz.

Shortly after 9:30 a.m. Drews, guarded by several officers, entered the courtroom, his head heavily bandaged. It was a dramatic moment and photographers responded accordingly, their flashbulbs popping wildly. At first sight of the defendant, shocked spectators erupted with gasps and excited speculation, which prompted Judge Duquaine to rap his gavel and order silence. Everyone was itching for the big event finally to begin, but the judge, wisely perhaps, instructed officers to take Drews for x-rays to determine if he could stand trial. When the crowd groaned their disappointment at the delay, Duquaine didn't even bother gaveling them.

Rowe and Dodd

The press was kept completely in the dark about Drews's she-nanigans at the jail, so they made wild stabs at the truth. "Suicide attempt by murder suspect" was their best guess. The truth was a secret well-kept by the Rowe family and a few officers. In a way, I wished the true story *had* made the news. DREWS'S ATTEMPTED JAILBREAK PROMPTLY THWARTED BY SHERIFF'S WIFE AND SON HARVEY!" was a headline I certainly could have lived with.

Anyway, when we pieced everything together, it seems Drews jumped from his top bunk headfirst onto the concrete floor, thus gashing his head. His plan was not to knock himself silly but to catch everyone off guard, perhaps slug it out with the sheriff or even his wife, and then flee. It was a pitiful scheme that failed miserably—instead of freedom, all he got was a splitting headache. He underesti-mated not only Mom but also the hardness of the concrete, the softness of his head, or both.

By 10:30 Drews was back in court to stand trial for first-degree murder. The case against Drews was so strong that his attorney, Frank Weis, had earlier urged him to plead guilty to any charge short of first-degree murder. Weis knew he could produce not even a single effec-tive witness for the defense and that his client faced a quick convic-tion. Drews rejected the advice, however, and took his chances.

The jury was selected from an initial panel of thirty-six persons from all parts of the county. After the two sides made their picks, the final panel consisted of ten men, two women, and an alternate. District Attorney Ed Minor sought to prove premeditation, and the best piece of evidence was Drews's sworn confession [see Appendix A]. The defense's only hope was to show that undue force had been used to extract the defendant's confession and that no evidence of premedita-tion existed.

Other than jury selection, little was accomplished in the morning. In the afternoon Judge Duquaine ordered a little exercise for the jury. He instructed them to walk two blocks for a tour the Cody mansion, with Sheriff Rowe as their guide. Drews was allowed to tag along. Attorney Weis declined to make the walk, though, due to a "bum leg."

After court resumed the judge swore in two bailiffs. My mother, Anna Rowe, would oversee the two women jurors, while Deputy Tom Christenson would take care of the men. The trial audience, which had waited all day for some action, was sorely disappointed when Duquaine announced that court was over for the day. Drews was returned to the jail at 4:14 p.m.

As usual the jurors and deputies had been admonished not to discuss the case. That evening the jury was treated to a stay at the "swanky" Hotel Swoboda in downtown Sturgeon Bay. To keep things from getting too rowdy, the two female jurors, accompanied by Mom, were assigned to a separate floor from the male jurors.

The second day of the trial began promptly at 9:00 a.m. on Wednesday, April 21. Defendant William Drews appeared anything but confident. As described by a reporter from the *Green Bay Press-Gazette,* "Drews did not exhibit the nonchalance that was evident at his arraignment. He fidgeted constantly yet did not appear to take any keen interest in the proceedings."

The prosecution called ten witnesses, including Loretta Burke, who described her concern for her missing friend and the eventual discovery of Mrs. Cody's body in the furnace. A farm loan agent disclosed that Drews had been in the process of purchasing a fourteen-acre farm fourteen miles north of Sturgeon Bay—all Drews had to do was come up with a $2000 down payment. Another witness testified he tried to help the defendant refinance his car, loaned him $10, and promised him a job. It seemed clear Drews had been in dire financial straits on the day of the murder.

By the time DA Ed Minor finished his case, the evidence seemed overwhelming. All Frank Weis had been able to do for his client was to make strategic objections and hope Judge Duquaine would sustain a few of them. The defense's goal was not acquittal but simply a reduced sentence, and their best chance was to show that Drews's written confession was coerced by Sheriff Rowe, who after all was a former neighbor and friend of Sadie Cody's. Here is part of Weis's cross-examination of the sheriff.

> Attorney Weis (Q): For many years you lived next door to Mrs. Cody, didn't you?
>
> Sheriff Rowe (A): Yes, sir.
>
> Q: How many years?
>
> A: About four.
>
> Q: You were neighbors and good friends, correct?
>
> A: Yes, sir.
>
> Q: You felt intensely about it when you found out she was killed, didn't you?
>
> A: Probably no more than any other person who had been murdered and I proceeded with the same intense investigation I would have with anyone else.
>
> Q: From the time you started questioning the defendant about Mrs. Cody, you really went after him to make him admit something, isn't that correct?
>
> A: Yes.
>
> Q: That's all.

That really *was* about all——the curtains were closing rapidly on William Drews. The medical doctors were questioned. Dr. John Muehlhauser stated his belief that Mrs. Cody was alive at the time she was placed in the furnace. Dr. Pessin, the pathologist, agreed, vividly acting out how Mrs. Cody's arms were positioned as if shielding her face from the intense flames of the furnace.

According to testimony, the firepot itself was only 30 x 30 in, and its door even smaller, 24 x 18 in. Cramming a body, even one as tiny as Mrs. Cody's, into the firepot would have taken some effort. Pessin testified that coal was found on top of the body, suggesting the defendant had "stoked the flames." In addition, an air vent was open to increase the fire's heat. Clearly the goal had been total incineration.

Finally the prosecution's case concluded. Now it was the defense's turn. The court spectators leaned forward, hoping Drews would take the stand to explain himself. Defense Attorney Weis astonished the crowd, however, when he abruptly announced that he would not call even a single witness for the defense. It was their right, of course—innocent until proven guilty—but the crowd was sorely disappointed.

That day in court, I paid attention as I never did in school. Ed Minor waxed eloquent in his closing argument, and I'll never forget one of his final remarks to the jury: "Remember Mrs. R. P. Cody. What will that old lady's tombstone read at Bayside Cemetery? It will read: *Murdered by William Drews. Burned alive on April 2, 1948!*"

That statement vividly reminded the jurors, as well as the spectators, of the final moments of agony in the life of Sadie Cody. There was a brief moment of silence in the courtroom, and I noticed that most people shifted their eyes to the blackboard still standing before the jury. On it was Dr. Pessin's hand-drawn image of Mrs. Cody as she lay in the firepot, her two frail hands extended as if to shield her face.

Minor must have noticed the shift in the audience's attention, too, as he once again pointed to the positioning of the victim's arms in the drawing and hammered home the point: "Those arms were Mrs. Cody's last feeble attempt to dispel the hungry flames that were devouring her still-alive and broken body." Weis objected but was overruled. Then Minor looked directly at Drews and told the jury he had committed this awful murder, "as cool as a cucumber."

At 4:15 p.m. the jury retired to deliberate the fate of William Drews. It took them only sixty-eight minutes. Judge Duquaine reconvened court for the final verdict, and Drews was once more brought to the courtroom from his jail cell. The huge audience scrambled for their seats. The verdict was quickly proclaimed: "Guilty of murder in the first degree."

A murmur of satisfaction rippled through the gallery, and heads nodded approvingly. The judge remanded Drews to the custody of Sheriff Rowe and announced that sentencing would be handed down on the following day. Justice was swift in 1948.

On Thursday, April 22, Judge Edward Duquaine ordered Williams Drews to stand. "Do you have anything to say before I impose sentence upon you?" "Not a thing," Drews replied. Those were the only three words he officially uttered during the two-day trial. Though he lost everything that day, he won the award for brevity. The judge ordered Drews to approach the bench and looked him directly in the eyes, their gazes locking. A moment later Judge imposed the maximum sentence—life imprisonment.

As Drews was escorted to the county jail, he expressed a desire to see his wife before departing for the state penitentiary. Showing a little sympathy, Sheriff Rowe called Julia Smith, the convict's bride of only three weeks, to ask if she'd come to the jail at 11:30 that morning. Initially she agreed but just before the appointed time, she called back to say she was sick and couldn't come.

At 1:00 p.m. that same day, Drews was transported by Sheriff Rowe and two officers to the Wisconsin state prison in Waupun, 130 miles away. At 3:15, Drews entered the stone walls of the maximum-security prison that would be his home for the rest of his life.

~ ~ ~

Dad and I saw Drews only once again. Many years after his conviction we were taking a walk through Waupun prison after delivering a prisoner. From a corner in the tailor shop, someone called out, "Hello, Hallie!" Dad turned to look and it was Bill Drews! Dad didn't know whether to smile or scowl, so he just offered a little "hi sign" with his hand, and I mimicked the gesture. Later we asked a guard how Drews was coping as an inmate, and we were surprised to learn he was a "model prisoner." Like most convicts, I suppose, he tried to stay focused on his ultimate goal—being paroled.

When Drews applied for parole in 1959, former DA Edward Minor, then U.S. Attorney in Wisconsin, vigorously opposed parole and asked Dad to join in his petition. Dad willingly aided in the effort. By that time Drews had served eleven years, and it was conceivable that he would receive parole. Quick interventions by Minor and Rowe, especially Minor's strongly worded letter, apparently convinced the parole board to deny Drews's petition for release. [Minor's letter to the board appears in Appendix B.]

Furnace Murder

The official jail register of Door County lists every booking of a prisoner. It provides a very interesting history of local crime, and throughout the years I spent many hours pouring over it. To me the most important prisoner of all was William Drews, and I committed to memory the notation in the "disposition" column beside his name: "Sentenced to Wis. State Prison for Life!" I was so impressed by the exclamation point that I searched every entry, forward and backwards. That exclamation point, so telling of the strong emotion that enveloped the case, is absolutely the only one that appears in the entire book, which dates back to 1887!

Coincidentally, 1887 was the year that a young, vivacious teacher named Sadie Marsh made her way from Oshkosh to Sturgeon Bay to teach school. One year later the *Door County Advocate* inserted a brief but poignant article about Sadie's marriage to R. P. Cody: "The *Advocate* extends the customary congratulations and trusts that the union so auspiciously begun may endure for many years."

17

Harvey's Epilogue

[What follows is the epilogue Harvey Rowe wrote to his original manuscript. It provides a fitting ending to the saga of Sadie E. Cody, as viewed through Harvey's eyes. It does not, however, include information that is often presented in an epilogue, including answers to such questions as: What happened to the Cody mansion? What became of Sheriff Rowe after he retired? Was Harvey Rowe ever able to move on with his life after those thrilling but perhaps terrifying years he spent living in the jail? I (DKD) have addressed questions such as these in the Afterword.]

Ours was the last sheriff's family to live in the old greystone jail. Ed Minor proposed that the building be converted into a joint city-county "safety building," an idea he got from his time in Milwaukee. Although Dad opposed it, the city and county agreed with Minor and in 1949 it became a reality.

At the end of December 1948, we packed up and moved back home, two blocks away and next door to the Cody mansion. After the murder, there just didn't seem to be anything that shocked me or, for that matter, motivated me. I didn't even care that we were moving from the jail.

After we returned to our house, the mansion seemed so dark and lifeless. From time to time, I would look out our window toward the stately old home next door. Somehow I always expected to see a ghostly figure of a little old lady—somewhere in a window or on the front porch—dressed in a pretty pink dress with little flowers adorning it, but it never happened, of course.

And *always*, when I looked out my bedroom window, my eyes would fix on that cellar window that so paradoxically admitted a sliver of sunshine into that awful furnace room. That window demonically captured me, forcing me to recall every ghastly detail of Mrs. Cody's death. Each time I would become overwhelmed and have to force myself to turn away.

Could her soul ever truly rest? And what about mine? One dream has always haunted me, certainly in my youth but even during my adult years. In the dark of night Mrs. Cody appears to me at the front door of her doomed mansion. With her tiny, frail voice, she speaks these few words that I have never been able to shake from my memory: "Can't you come in and talk with me? Stay for a few minutes and visit."

Cody mansion as viewed from south.
Rowe home is just left of mansion.

Cody mansion, c. 1948, viewed from north.

Sadie Marsh Cody

About age 48 (c. 1910),
wearing favorite fur coat.

Undated photo, near the
end of her life.

Jail *(L)* while Harvey Rowe was in residence, and courthouse (c. 1945).

Jail and courthouse in 1909.

Harvey Rowe, age 14, in his "study."

Six-year-old Harvey, pulling his sled in Garland Park, Sturgeon Bay, WI.

Sheriff Hallie Rowe

Undersheriff Christianson "on duty."
Note bulletin board meticulously maintained by Harvey Rowe.

Mansion's parlor, where Drews requested a loan from Mrs. Cody. Her beloved fur coat, a gift from her husband decades earlier, is on the chair back. The hatchet on the wall symbolizes Mrs. Cody's claim that she was a cousin by marriage to Wild Bill Cody.

Right: Mrs. Cody's "day bed," where she slept at night, surrounded by R.P. Cody's law books. Notice mattress sagging from years of use.

Blood droplets on bathroom sink.

Bloody mess in bathtub.

Remains of Sadie Cody in firepot, lying on her back, feet to the right. Arrow points to skull. Stoker switch (thermostat) is left of skull. Evidence shows Drews "stoked" the fire, though he denied it.

Sheriff Rowe begins removing bones from furnace firepot.

Pathologist Samuel Pessin organizes bones on a schema.

"Crime Doctor" Charles Wilson dusts for prints, endlessly.

Circuit Court Judge Edward S. Duquaine, who presided over Drews's trial.

William Drews at his arraignment on April 7, appearing
calm and collected, possibly contrite. At his trial on
April 20, his appearance was drastically different.

Left: William Drews escorted into the courtroom on April 20. His head is bandaged from a fall in his cell earlier that morning. Some called it a suicide attempt, others an attempted jailbreak. His escorts are Deputy Jack Pivonka (L) and Officer Joseph Antonissen (R).

Right: Who's in charge? Photographer Herb Reynolds captures a lighter moment at trial. Sheriff Rowe points to Undersheriff Thomas Christianson while Deputy Pivonka looks on. The chagrined defendant holds his weary, bandaged head.

Behind the defendant sits two key witnesses for the prosecution: Loretta Burke (hands folded) and Alice McLaughlin (arms folded). The two women were neighbors and close friends of Mrs. Cody's.

Pathologist Samuel Pessin demonstrates to the jury that Mrs. Cody was alive at the time she was shoved into the furnace. The positioning of the hands seems to suggest the victim was shielding her face from the flames.

Attending the trial were Drews's second wife Julia Smith (right)
and her daughter Eileen (left). It is unclear whether Mrs. Smith
was rooting for or against her new husband, but shortly after
the trial she had her marriage to Drews annulled.

Wisconsin State Prison

Waupun, Wis. April 22, 19 48

Received from the Sheriff of ___ DOOR ___ County, the following

named convict sentenced by the ___ Circuit ___ Court for County of

___ Door ___ to-wit:

___ William Drews #30042 ___ sentenced ___ 4/22/48 ___ 19___

___ for a term of ___ LIFE ___

John C. Burke
Warden.

On April 21, Drews was convicted of murder. The next morning, he was
sentenced to life in prison, and by that afternoon he began serving his time
at Wisconsin State Prison in Waupun.

One of two rental properties owned by Mrs. Cody in 1948. This one is on E. Oak St. William Drews and Julia Smith lived in the one on N. Sixth Ave. – it is no longer standing. Monthly rent was about $25.00. Tenants complained about run-down conditions.

The Greystone Castle, a historical landmark, has been a popular bar in Sturgeon Bay for many decades. William Drews married Julia Smith one day after the Cody murder. The happy couple, one of whom was unaware of the killing, celebrated into the night at the Greystone.

HALLIE ROWE

—— for ——

SHERIFF

of Door County on the Republican Ticket
15 years experience in law enforcement as game
warden in Door County . . . Served in World
War I . . . 18 months overseas . . . Member of
American Legion.

YOUR VOTE WILL BE APPRECIATED AT
THE PRIMARY TUESDAY, AUGUST 15, 1944

(Authorized and circulated by Hallie Rowe,
22 N. 5th Street, Sturgeon Bay, Wis.)

Hallie Rowe's first campaign card,
1944. He ran for sheriff five times
and was successful each time!

Harvey also ran for state and local
offices but never won. In the middle
is a deputy sheriff's badge. It may
have been given to Harvey during
childhood, or later in life. He had a
lifelong fascination with law
enforcement.

Graves of Sadie, Richard, and Irene Cody (L-R) at Bayside Cemetery, Sturgeon Bay, WI. Not far from Sadie are the graves of: Hallie, Anna, and Harvey Rowe; trusted advisor and lawyer William E. Wagener; town photographer Herb Reynolds; and friend and neighbor Allie McLaughlin.

Grave of Harvey Rowe

Mrs. Cody bequeathed $1000 for a town clock. It was erected on the old fire house (now a restaurant), adjacent to the old city hall (now a visitor's bureau). The clock still "runs" but hasn't kept correct time in years. No one seems to care about having it fixed.

The inscription (on wall below clock) is still in good shape, though most town visitors, or even many residents, do not recognize the Cody name.

Harvey Rowe, displaying two passions – motorcycles and license plates.

Part IV

18

Mysterious Death of Margaret Drews

In October 1929 the U.S. economy "crashed" on Black Tuesday. The result was a severe worldwide economic depression that dominated the decade leading up to World War II. In the U.S. the Great Depression produced crippling unemployment that reached 25% by 1933 and suppressed farm prices by 60%. It was not a good time to be poor, a farmer, or especially both.

Margaret Long was born in 1911 in a small farming community in central Wisconsin. Though only seventeen, she was determined to marry William Drews, despite the dire economic news that was sweeping the nation. Bill, a local farmer who was her senior by fourteen years, was already accustomed to hard times and probably owned not a single share of stock. Margaret might not have even known what stock was. Three weeks after Black Tuesday, Margaret turned eighteen and immediately plunged into marriage with Bill.

On the evening of March 16, 1946, Margaret died, not far from her home among the apple orchards near Sturgeon Bay. Her body was found completely incinerated in the passenger seat of an automobile that had crashed. The most obvious explanation was that an accident had occurred, igniting the car in flames, and Margaret's death was due either to the crash or the resulting fire. But competing explanations, or theories, exist.

The driver of the car was Bill Drews, her husband. A responding police offer reported finding him near the scene, wandering around in an apparent daze. The severity of his injuries is unclear, though he was hospitalized for approximately five days.

Drews later told police that he and his wife left home at about 9:40 p.m. for a dance sponsored by the Odd Fellows Lodge. They had been looking forward to the event for weeks. Although they themselves were not members, they had attended dances several times in the past under the Lodge membership of close friends.

From their home north of Sturgeon Bay, the couple drove west toward the bay before turning south onto Bay Shore Drive and heading toward town. Bill Drews would later report that at 9:45 p.m., only five minutes after departing from their home, a rear tire blew out. He lost control and ended up in the woods, where he crashed among a grove of trees not far from the Sandy Bay Cottages resort. Drews claimed that both he and his wife were rendered unconscious.

Even the most basic facts of the event are in dispute, including when the wreckage was discovered, who discovered it, and who called the fire department to put out the car blaze. Several "eyewitnesses" to the aftermath of the crash told wildly varying stories, which conflicted with newspaper accounts of the accident.

The *Door County Advocate* story was headlined: "Woman is Killed When Blowout Ditches Auto," with a subheading of: "Husband is Pulled to Safety as Fire Results from Crash." According to the newspaper the accident occurred at 9:45 p.m., but the car fire was not noticed until about 10:45 p.m., when an unspecified witness at the scene called the Sturgeon Bay Fire Department for help. Unfortunately the department was under standing orders not to respond to fires outside the city unless prior agreements had been made with the township.

Hearing the distress call over the police radio, Traffic Officer Eldon Carmody responded to scene and made a "complete investigation," although no official report can be located. It was presumably Carmody who insisted that a fire unit be dispatched, despite the standing order. The *Advocate* credited two local servicemen with being the first to detect the burning car, though the actual number might have been three. According to the *Milwaukee Sentinel,* the men pulled

Furnace Murder

Bill Drews from the car but could not rescue Margaret due to the intensity of the fire. Later they talked about what they found.

According to the servicemen they attended a movie in Sturgeon Bay that evening and sometime after 9:00 p.m. decided to take a ride along Bay Shore Drive. They traveled several miles north before turning around and heading back toward town. On their way back, at a spot they had passed just minutes earlier, they came upon a burning vehicle about a hundred feet off the road. They stopped to investigate.

Fifty years after the event fatal event, one of the men recounted what he observed. Unfortunately, but perhaps predictably, his account conflicts starkly with what the *Sentinel* reported: "We saw the car burning down in the woods, away from the ditch, and we went up to it, not real close as we were concerned about the gas tank exploding. The entire car was enveloped in flames and at least one door was open. One of us went around to the other side, and there was absolutely no evidence of a body. Nobody in the car. Nothing."

This witness recalled two critical "facts": The car was neither up against a tree nor wedged between two trees, and one or two doors were open at the time. The servicemen got back into their car and drove into town, where they reported the accident to city police. The officer who took their report did not seem to believe them—in any event, the accident was outside of the city and thus not under the jurisdiction of the city police. The witness was shocked to learn the next day that a woman had burned to death in the car.

Another person claimed, also more than fifty years later, to have witnessed the accident scene. Having finished his supper at the Shipmate Tavern sometime between 7:30 and 8:30 that evening, he spotted a car in the woods and got out to look around. "I did not look in the car, I just assumed that someone had already gone for help." What puzzled him was, "Who would drive in there like that?" And he did not see any fire.

There were others who claimed to be eyewitnesses. A man and his wife, along with another couple, were driving north on Bay Shore Drive, their goal being dinner at the popular Shipmate Tavern. Spotting the burning car, they stopped to investigate and claimed that there was no officer at the scene. This witness remembers: "Drews was lying on the shoulder of the road, quite a ways from the blazing vehicle, which was wedged between two trees." He further recalled that the driver's side door especially could not have been opened as it was pinned tightly against a tree. He claims Drews was conscious at the scene.

Back to the *Advocate's* report: "The Drewses left their home at about 9:40 p.m. and the crash occurred about five minutes later . . . . It was not until 10:45 that a passerby noticed the fire and called it in." Official fire department records show, however, that the call was received not at 10:45 p.m. but nearly two hours later, at 12:35 a.m. One truck was dispatched and, after remaining at the scene only twenty minutes, returned to the station at 1:20 a.m.

In short, four glaring inconsistencies in the "facts" of the accident must be considered. First, the timeline: Drews reports that the crash happened about five minutes after he left home at 9:40 p.m. A newspaper report suggests that a car fire was not reported until about 10:45, but the fire department reports first receiving the call at 12:30 a.m. The two couples who witnessed the blaze were "heading to dinner"—but surely that could not have been after midnight! Sometime that night two, or three, servicemen arrived at the scene and either pulled Bill Drews from the car or saw absolutely no one.

Second, was the car jammed between two trees, or not? Some witnesses say yes, others report no such thing. Some say one or two car doors were even wide open.

The third discrepancy is the nature of the fire that engulfed the car. The police officer on the scene claimed, "I could see [the victim] sitting in there. The damn thing was going like hell. I couldn't get close." Others saw the disabled car but no sign of a fire. Ed Minor, the District Attorney himself, weighed in. From his 1959 letter to Drews's parole board [see Appendix B]: "Evidence we obtained after his conviction was that he also murdered his first wife inasmuch as her car was found alongside a road amongst some trees and was burned, the car having been burned only on the side where she had been sitting." And then there is the report in the *Advocate:* "The car was so far gone that the door on Mrs. Drews's side had opened and the body had partially fallen out . . . . The car was almost a total wreck, everything burned but the front tires. The rear tires were gone, so it was impossible to determine which one blew out and caused Mr. Drews to lose control."

Finally, it is not clear whether Drews was conscious and walking around at the scene, or unconscious. One witness remembered that Drews was "fully conscious and knew what happened." The *Advocate*, however, reported that Drews was found "lying unconscious about six feet away. He did not regain his senses until he reached the hospital. His first words were, 'Did anyone save my wife?'" And the servicemen—did they pull Drews from the car or did they find absolutely no one at the scene?

These then are the details of the crash in the woods, as remembered quite disparately by the many witnesses. More important, perhaps, to understanding what might have happened that night are the dynamics of the Drews family.

Although Margaret Drews died in 1946, it was not until twenty-five months later, after Mrs. Cody had been murdered and Bill Drews was awaiting trial, that an official inquiry into Margaret's death began. Drews's oldest daughter Audrey, who was fifteen at the time of the her mother's death but seventeen at the time of her interview, was interrogated in depth by two investigators about the events surrounding that tragic night. The exact date of the interview is unknown, except that it occurred sometime between Drews's confession to Mrs. Cody's murder (April 6) and his conviction (April 22). The interview took place in the small community where Audrey was living with relatives, about a hundred miles from Sturgeon Bay.

Below is the complete transcript of the interview, which in its original form was twenty-two handwritten pages. It reveals a lot about the Drews family, especially about the dynamics of the household on the evening that Margaret died. What it does not reveal, unfortunately, is what direct role, if any, Bill played in his wife's death.

Investigator (I): How old are you?
Audrey (A): Seventeen.
I: You lived in Sturgeon Bay with your dad and mother?

A: Yes. We moved up here in June 1942.

I: Where did you live then?

A: At Martin Orchards.

I: Where did your dad work?

A: At [the shipbuilders].

I: In March 1946 where were you living?

A: In a house near Goldman Orchards.

I: And where was your father working then?

A: For May's Gas Service, for about four years.

I: Now, did your dad and your mother get along, or were they having a little trouble?

A: There was never anything said—but he wasn't home too much. At first everything was all right, but, I don't know—he just wasn't home very much. Mother never complained. She didn't argue, didn't say anything. She'd just keep it all to herself. I can't ever remember them having any arguments.

I: Do you recall your dad perhaps seeing another woman?

A: I never saw him—but I'd always heard. . . . I knew, because he was never home—and there's nothing else to think.

I: Do you remember the names of any women?

A: No, I'd never heard any names. Only this Julia was about the only one I ever heard about.

I: Did you know about her?

A: Um-hum.

I: And how about Julia? She was married to a Mr. Smith, wasn't she?

A: That's what I understand.

I: And where did she live, in relation to your house. Did she live near you?

A: No, she didn't live near us. I never knew that he was seeing her while my mother was alive. I didn't know her name or anything, but people had told me—long afterward—that she was the one that he had been seeing.

I: Did you have some idea, while your mother was living, he was seeing this Julia, is that your understanding?

A (after a pause): Yes.

Furnace Murder

I: Did you ever hear your mother say anything to him about that?

A: No.

I: There was never any discussion at home that you over-heard?

A: If there had been, I think it would have been said so that my sister and I wouldn't have heard anything.

I: Was your dad nice to you children?

A: Oh, yes, we couldn't ask for a better father.

I: Now, getting back to the time just before the death of your mother, did your mother go out to dance with your father regularly? Was that an ordinary thing?

A: They were invited out to these Odd Fellow dances by their friends, and they always went.

I: Did they go together?

A: Um-hum.

I: That was quite usual?

A: Um-hum.

I: Do you happen to know where they were going the night that your mother was killed?

A: To the Odd Fellows dance.

I: Do you remember that morning, what happened?

A: No.

I: Is there anything in your memory about that morning that stands out?

A: No. I don't remember a thing until that evening.

I: What time of day did the accident take place, according to your understanding?

A: About 10:30 [p.m.].

I: As far as you can remember, what happened that day before the accident? Were you at home or away?

A: I was at home until about 7:00 [p.m.].

I: And how were things around home that day? Were they about the same or was there anything unusual.

A: I didn't notice anything unusual.

I: Would you say there was tension in the air that day?

A: Not that I noticed.

I: Had there been any talk about you girls going someplace for the evening, or something of that nature?

A: Well, I had that evening planned. I was going to a party, and I was staying with my girlfriend.

I: And where was your little sister to stay?

A: At friends, up at Martin Orchards.

I: And that had already been previously planned? And was your mother, as far as you can remember, looking forward to this dance—as an outing for herself?

A: Well, it had been planned earlier in the week.

I: It wasn't something that came up in a hurry?

A: No.

I: Now, you left home about 7:00 that night?

A: As closely as I remember.

I: And your little sister left home when?

A: We all left at the same time, but they took me over to my girlfriend's first.

I: You said "they"—you mean your mother and your dad?

A: Yes.

I: And how were things between them? Did they seem to be in good spirits?

A: Yes.

I: Were they talking together?

A: Sure.

I: Did there seem to be anything between them the last time you saw them?

A: No, nothing I could put my finger on.

I: In other words, they were friendly and getting along that night, just like any other night?

A: Yes.

I: And they took you over to your girlfriend's and left you off and that's the last you saw your mother alive?

A (softly, nearly inaudibly): The last time.

I: Now, had your mother ever expressed any fear of your father?

A: No.

I: You kids, were you afraid of him?

A: No, I was not. I wasn't afraid to do anything around him.

Furnace Murder

I: When did you first hear about the death of your mother?

A: The next morning.

I: What was it you heard the next morning and who did you hear it from?

A: [A family friend] came to my girlfriend's, where I was staying, and told me that there had been an accident and then he took me down to May's [Drews's employer]—and they didn't say anything except that Dad had been hurt. I was so struck I didn't think to ask about my mother or anything. And then they told me that she had been killed.

I: And how soon did you see your father?

A: Not until that same afternoon. I went up to the hospital to see him.

I: What was his condition then?

A: I don't remember really, but I think he was supposed to have had a bandage on his head and broken ribs.

I: And were there any *visible* signs of injury on him? He had some scratches on his face that I understand.

A: That's what I understood too. But I didn't really notice it.

I: Getting back to the time when they left you off at your girlfriend's, did they go directly to the dance?

A: No. They had to take my little sister and then had to go home to dress, because they weren't dressed yet.

I: So they wouldn't have left for the dance for some two to three hours after they left you off?

A: That's right.

I: When he was in the hospital, did you see any signs of scratches on his face?

A: I only saw him there once or twice and then I didn't pay any attention to anything like that.

I: Did he appear to be hurt?

A: I don't remember. I just took it for granted, since he was in the hospital.

I: Did he tell you how the accident happened?

A: No, he didn't say anything. What I heard I always heard from somebody else.

I: Well, didn't you discuss how it happened with him?

A: He told me that he had a flat tire and [inaudible].

I: Did he tell you that?

A: I think he did when there was others around, but—I never talked to him.

I: What was the first thing he said to you when you walked into the hospital room? Can you remember? Did he seem glad to see you?

A: He put his arms around me, I remember that.

I: Did he seem pretty much broken up about the accident?

A: He did.

I: He didn't have anything to say about how it happened or anything else? Did he tell you that it [your mother's death] had happened?

A: Yes, he had said—no, I don't believe he did [say anything] because they didn't tell him until the next day.

I: In other words, your recollection is that your father didn't know that your mother was dead at that time, is that it?

A: I can't remember. I don't remember if the doctor had told him then or not.

I: In other words, you don't know whether your dad—?

A: No. I can't remember.

I: He never mentioned the death of your mother to you, is that it? Do I have that straight?

A: He didn't say anything in the hospital that day.

I: The first time you saw him, he didn't have anything to say about the death of your mother? He just put his arms around you?

A: That's right.

I: That's as far as you can remember. Now, how long did you stay in there that first time?

A: Ten minutes, that was about all.

I: And when was the next time you saw him?

A (after a long pause): I don't think I saw him until after the funeral. Because I came up here [to another community some distance from Sturgeon Bay] to stay, and . . .

I: You came up here how long after the accident?

Furnace Murder

A: I can't remember. I got that all mixed up. I came up here on the day of the funeral. Before the funeral, I stayed in Sturgeon Bay with my girlfriend.

I: About how many days were there from the date of the death until the funeral?

A: The funeral was on Wednesday, or Thursday—it was Wednesday—and the accident was on Saturday night.

I: Was your dad still in the hospital?

A: He was until the day of the funeral.

I: Did he come to the funeral?

A: No, he didn't.

I: Do you have any idea why he didn't come?

A: I thought he was too sick or something, but he was released that afternoon.

I: So you don't know whether he *could* have come or not?

A: I think he could have.

I: And do you have any idea why he didn't come?

A: No.

I: He just didn't come?

A: Didn't come.

I: Were you surprised at that, or is that consistent with the way he would always act?

A (after long pause): Well, at the time I didn't think too much about it, because I was under the impression that he was quite ill.

I: Did you see your father after the funeral?

A: Not right after it.

I: When was the first time you saw him after the funeral?

A: I don't remember.

I: Were you close to your father, so that you would sit down and have a talk with him? Were you that close to him, or weren't you?

A: No. It seemed afterwards—I don't know if it was my imagination but—I hadn't talked to him too much lately, and I didn't tell him any of my troubles or anything. But afterwards I just couldn't talk to him very good, it didn't seem.

I: Was it that he didn't have time, or was he reluctant to talk about things in his past with your mother, or . . . ?

A: Well, I didn't like to talk about it either, so I guess neither one of us talked about it.

I: Did he ever tell you why he didn't come to the funeral?

A: No, we never talked about it.

I: He never made any apology or anything of that nature? Never told you that he was sick, or that he wasn't sick, or that something else prevented him? No explanation?

A: No. Never talked about it.

I: Did you have the occasion to talk to him [in the months following the accident]?

A: I hadn't seen him since [September], not to talk to him really.

I: And when did you see him then, in September?

A: That was before I moved up here [to live with relatives].

I: Oh, I see. You hadn't seen him since September?

A: Yes, he came up here a number of times, but he always just came and went. [Drews visited the community where he had relatives and where Audrey was living.]

I: Did he ever stop to see you when he came?

A: Oh, yes.

I: What would he have to say when he did see you?

A: Well, what he had been doing, but oh, we found out later it wasn't the truth what he did tell me, especially the last time he was here, he said he was working when he [really] wasn't.

I: Did he tell you that he was going to get married?

A: No, he never said anything about it. We always had the impression that he was already married but never told us.

I: I see. And you were of the impression that it was this Mrs. Smith—Julia Smith?

A: Yes.

I: Did you see him when he was up here on Monday, April 5 [1948, three days after Mrs. Cody's murder]. You know he was up here then, don't you?

A: I didn't know about it at the time.

Furnace Murder

I: He didn't stop to see you?

A: No.

I: Does he write to you?

A: He hasn't for a long time.

I: Did he before [the Cody murder]?

A: He'd always send us cards saying when he'd come, but then he never did come when he said he was going to—and I didn't care if he wrote anymore or not, I was so disgusted.

I: This is an awful thing to ask you, I know, but I gotta do it. What do you think about this accident and your mother? Was that an accident, or, I know you don't know . . . we don't know either. What do you think? Now you were home there, and I know it's an awful thing to ask you, but what do you think about it?

A: I guess I always did think there was something funny about it, but I never was, I never thought that he could do anything like that, so I just sort of put it in the back of my mind and never thought about it too much.

I: There isn't anything that you can lay your finger on and say that this is what makes it seem funny?

A: No, there's nothing.

I: It's just sort of a feeling that you have? Was your father a pretty good driver?

A: I'd say he was average.

I: Was he a fellow who was cool in an emergency or did he get flustered very easily? Have you ever been in the car with him when something came up unexpectedly and he had to make a quick decision to keep from hitting something?

A: Well, he was pretty calm.

I: Now, what's his temperament ordinarily? Was he pretty calm at all times or nervous and excitable?

A: I think he was always pretty calm. He never got upset real easily or anything that I ever noticed.

I: You know, of course, what he's accused of doing up in Sturgeon Bay, is that [the killing of Mrs. Cody] consistent with your knowing him?

Rowe and Dodd

A: No. I still don't know how—.

I: It's hard for you to conceive of his doing [inaudible] and except for his confession, you'd believe it?

A: Yes.

I (addressing another detective): You have anything?

Second detective (D): Did you notice the shoes your mother was wearing when she went to the dance? Were they regular house shoes or . . . ?

A: No, I don't know.

D: They were a good pair of shoes?

A: They must have been.

D: Do you ever recall making the statement that you thought it was funny that she was wearing old shoes?

A: No, I never said that.

D: Did your dad ever have trouble with tires on his car, prior to that accident?

A: He had flat tires occasionally.

First investigator (I): What clothes was your mother wearing to the dance that night? I mean, could you tell by what was missing in the house?

A: Yes, she had on a black dress.

I: Was that a good dress?

A: Yes.

I: And the shoes that were left at home—were her good shoes missing?

A: Yes, there was a pair of black shoes missing, too.

I: There *were?* You know, positively, that she had on her good shoes?

A: Yeah. She must have because there was one pair that I never saw after that.

I: From the things that were gone [from the house] that belonged to her, you would assume that she was dressed up nice, to go somewhere?

A: Yes.

I: Were you ever back in the house after the death of your mother?

A: Yes, the following day.

Furnace Murder

I: Do you recall whether or not there were any signs of a struggle around the house, or outside?

A: No.

I: Were any gasoline cans missing, something of that nature?

A: No.

I: Did you have gasoline around the place, or kerosene?

A: Kerosene.

I: And how much did you have around? Cases?

A: Yes. We had cans, too.

I: How many kerosene cans did you have?

A: I think there were two larger ones and one smaller one.

I: And do you know whether that car had ever caught fire before, not by itself?

A: No.

I: As far as you know, it had never caught on fire from any cause? And you wouldn't know, of course, whether there were any kerosene cans missing?

A: No. I don't know.

I: Now, is there anything that you know about this, Audrey, that you think we ought to know?

A: Well, there's nothing that I know really about it, except what everyone has told me. But when we were up there [in Sturgeon Bay] and my uncle was talking to the sheriff, he told things that I had never heard before about puddles of blood being outside and—.

I: Did you see any blood outside?

A: No. I wasn't looking for any and if there would have been, I wouldn't have seen it anyhow.

I: Do you have chickens on the farm that you had?

D: Did your father ever kill any chickens around home?

A: No, not at that time. I don't remember if there were any chickens there then, but there had been before.

I: You hadn't had chicken to eat several days before?

A: No.

I: Did you go down and look where the accident happened?

A: Yes.

I: What did you see as far as an actual layout of the car and everything? What did it look like to you?

143

[There is a break in the transcript. Perhaps the question was withdrawn.]

    I: Has your little sister ever made any remarks to you about the relationship of your father and mother? Has she ever told you anything?

    A: No.

    D: Did your mother ever meet this Mrs. Smith?

    A: I don't think so.

    D: Did you ever hear your dad talking about her?

    A: No, I never heard her name mentioned or anything.

    I: There was never any arguments at home about his going around with Mrs. Smith?

    A: No.

    I: Would you say it was a happy home life that you had?

    A: Well, I was always quite happy except that he was never home. I mean, things—.

    I: Did your mother seem to be satisfied with things the way they were? Or resigned to be tough, was that it?

    A: She just seemed to realize that there was nothing to do about it, and—.

    I: Whatever was wrong, it had to be that way?

    A: She wrote and told my aunt that she had planned on leaving him though, as soon as I was through school. I don't know if she meant through for good [done with high school] or just for that year.

    I: Did she ever discuss any of this with you?

    A: No.

[End of interview.]

19

Who was the Real William Drews?

Harvey Rowe had very strong opinions about William Drews, and he expressed them vigorously throughout his original manuscript: *William Drews was a cold-blooded, vicious, sociopathic, serial killer.* His hatred for Drews seemed at times to be truly unrestrained.

As I [DKD] have tried to get to know my coauthor through his manuscript, it is clear to me that, like many people, Harvey saw the world as black and white, good versus evil, law-abiding or law-offending. To Harvey, Hallie Rowe was not merely a father but the greatest force for goodness in the universe, the ultimate protector of the law. And Bill Drews was not only the villain that took Mrs. Cody's life but also the outlaw who singularly challenged, and ultimately defined, Sheriff Rowe's reputation as sheriff. Without question the actions of Drews during the brief time he was in the Cody mansion on that fateful Friday in 1948 were despicable. Nevertheless Harvey Rowe took the ball of blame and ran with it far beyond the criminal act, projecting those few heinous moments onto Drews's entire adult life.

Does the evidence support Harvey's claim that Drews was a cold-blooded, sociopathic serial killer? In order to answer in the affirmative, there would have to be at least two murders, both deliberate and pre-meditated. Was this the case?

Did Drews plan to kill Mrs. Cody in order to rob her?
Drews confessed to some horrible things but never admitted planning to kill Mrs. Cody, or even rob her. If his confession is to be believed, Drews aggressed on the victim only *after* she refused his request for a

loan. As I speculated in Chapter 11, Sadie Cody might have provoked Drews with a snide remark about the death of his first wife. Such provocation in no way justifies Drews's reaction, of course, but it does provide an alternative to the idea that his attack was premeditated.

There are several reasons to doubt that Drews schemed to rob and kill Mrs. Cody. Why would he park his car practically in front of the mansion in a residential neighborhood, walk to the front door, and stand there knocking, all in full daylight? And shortly thereafter, exit the house and return to his car in a similar manner? Wouldn't he have brought a murder weapon? Worn gloves to avoid leaving fingerprints, instead of desperately employing Sadie's nightcap to wipe away evidence?

The more logical scenario, in my view, is that Drews went to the mansion that day intending to ask Mrs. Cody for a small loan to fund his wedding celebration, if not a larger loan to purchase a farm. At his trial, a prosecution witness testified that Drews had been in the process of purchasing a farm for $5700, including a down payment of $2000. A news reporter quoted Julia Smith as saying that she and Drews had a farm "all spoken for." The newly married couple, along with Smith's four children, were planning to live on the land and make a go at farming. All Drews had to do was come up with the down payment.

A lot was riding on Drews that morning when he asked Mrs. Cody for financial help. Perhaps he pleaded with her, even begged for a loan. She steadfastly turned him down, possibly taunted him. He struck out in anger, then immediately realized that his future—certainly his wedding the next day—would be ruined if she regained consciousness and called the police. Everything afterwards was frantic cover-up.

Did Drews plot the death of his wife?

The circumstances surrounding the death of Margaret Drews seem odd at best, and highly suspicious at worst. There were rumors—how convenient that Drews's wife would be killed, leaving him free to openly pursue his relationship with Julia Smith. Something seemed "fishy" about the accident, because Margaret died in a horrific car fire while Bill escaped with injuries that were not life-threatening, though he was hospitalized for several days. An inquest was even held, but no criminal charges were levied—the matter was quietly dropped.

There is no reliable evidence that Drews deliberately killed his wife. First, there seems to be no motive. Though rumors about Drews's affair with Julia Smith were widespread, Margaret had not openly confronted her husband about it and had expressed no confirmable desire to end their marriage. Had love been his motive, why wait twenty-five months after the death of his first wife to marry Julia?

Second, if Drews coolly planned the murder, he chose a very odd place to stage a car accident. The scene of the wreck was just off a main road near a popular nightspot on a Saturday evening—a heavily traveled location that virtually guaranteed eyewitnesses to the event or its aftermath. Did Drews deliberately drive his car into a grove of trees, inflict himself with broken ribs and wounds to his head and face, douse the car with an accelerant, and set it ablaze? If so, he ran a terrible risk of being seen. How much more logical it would have been to choose a deserted location closer to their rural home. Bill could have staged the accident scene without any detection, walked home, and hours later called in a missing person's report, claiming that Margaret herself had driven away from home after an argument.

Third, Drews allegedly admitted to killing his wife, but that claim is highly suspect. According to Harvey Rowe, this "confession" was given verbally to Sheriff Rowe on the night of April 6. It had been a long, exhausting day for Drews even before the sheriff took him to jail—he had been apprehended and grilled for several hours at City Hall before eventually confessing to the Cody murder. Now the sheriff was back at it, browbeating him for a second confession. A short time later Sheriff emerged from the cellblock and announced "he confessed to the murder of his first wife!" Yet there were no witnesses, nothing in writing or on audiotape. Today we assume that confessions are preceded by a reading of the suspect's rights, but the *Miranda* warning now so basic to criminal interrogation did not exist at the time.

According to Harvey's account, minutes after Sheriff Rowe announced Drews's "second confession," a minister appeared on the scene and entered the jail to visit Drews. The implication is that Drews had requested to meet with a clergy, but that is not certain. Perhaps the minister's visit had been arranged by Sheriff Rowe to support the claim of a second confession. In any event, when the minister emerged from the jail, he, too, announced that Drews had confessed to murdering his first wife. It is important to note that no independent verification of this jailhouse confession exists. Whatever Drews might have said to the minister was passed along to Sheriff Rowe, who presumably told Harvey, perhaps years later. Interpretation, as well as the passage of time, can badly distort word-of-mouth information.

For example, what exactly did the sheriff, or the minister, ask Drews in his jail cell: *Were you involved in the death of your wife?* or *Did you murder your wife?* These are two very different questions. No one will ever really know exactly what was asked, how Drews responded, and why he responded as he did. Perhaps at that point, after many hours of questioning and accusations, he just threw in the proverbial towel.

What really happened the night Margaret Drews died?

Several possible scenarios exist. One, perhaps there really was a freak accident resulting from a blown-out tire. That was Bill's explanation, and it is supported by his broken ribs and other injuries that required hospitalization.

Two, it is conceivable that Bill and Margaret had an intense argument either prior to getting into their car or as they drove to Sturgeon Bay. Bill's driving might have been impaired due to the fight, and the result was the accident.

Three, it is possible that a violent confrontation at home resulted in a deadly blow and that Bill panicked, just as he might have done two years later in the Cody mansion. He might have grabbed a can of kerosene and headed out into the dark night, scheming, even as he drove, of a way to get rid of his wife's body.

None of these scenarios is very satisfying, because all are so highly speculative. But so is the alternative explanation that Drews deliberately and cold-heartedly planned and executed the murder of his wife. Ultimately, it is up to each reader to decide whether Drews was a cold-blooded killer or, alternatively, an unwitting player caught up in tragic circumstances.

Furnace Murder

Experts in violence distinguish two kinds of human aggression. The first type is proactive or instrumental and refers to actions focused on acquiring some goal, such as financial gain. Usually it is carefully planned to minimize the chance of detection, and often there is little if any emotion involved. This kind of aggression is "cool, calm, and collected."

The second type of aggression is much different. Reactive, or emotional, aggression involves little or no planning. It occurs in a social situation that evokes strong emotion in the aggressor, who then acts while in a state of impaired reasoning. Often the scenario involves a volatile encounter, a striking out, and finally a desperate, ineffective attempt to cover up the action. By now it should be no secret that Harvey Rowe and I have diametrically opposing explanations for William Drews's deadly behavior, as different as cold and hot.

What was Drews's temperament?

Was he cold and calculating, or an emotional person prone to violent outbursts? Unfortunately, there is very little information to answer that question. If he were alive today, Drews would be more than 120 years old! Any adult who knew him at the time of the Cody murder is now either deceased or extremely old. What is known, partly from the psychiatric evaluation of him shortly after his arrival at state prison in 1948 (see Appendix C), was that he was of normal intelligence and had never been charged with or convicted of any crime prior to the Cody case. He admitted to the prison psychiatrist one legal transgression: He felt he and his coworkers were being unfairly treated by their employer—cheated out of earnings—and in retaliation he stole $80. Apparently he was found out and promptly fired.

His father was a poor farmer, and Drews dropped out of school after the eighth grade, probably to help on the farm. He did not marry until age thirty-one. Despite occasional, brief periods of unemployment, Drews worked steadily to support his family. Although not wealthy, he and his wife formed a friendship with at least one prominent couple of the Sturgeon Bay community, with whom they socialized periodically. He was depicted by acquaintances as a pleasant, reasonably social individual who was well-liked. Julia Smith and her children were shocked when Drews was accused of killing Mrs. Cody. To them, Bill was "good, generous, and kind."

Two people still living knew Bill Drews intimately, and fortunately they were willing to speak to me. Only fifteen and six at the time their mother died, Drews's two daughters shared their thoughts, feelings, and ambivalence about their father nearly seventy years later. Today, Audrey and Patsy—now Pat—live in separate, rural communities within a few miles of each other. It is the same area where they were born and raised, as were both of their parents. Local residents are well aware of the deplorable fates of Bill and Margaret Drews, but Audrey and Pat have always maintained active social lives among wide circles of friends. They are close to their children, grandchildren, and great-grandchildren and enjoy holiday celebrations with their extended families.

It is hard to imagine the pain they, as girls, endured after the fiery death of their mother and, two years later, their father's conviction for the murder of Mrs. Cody. Following these tragic events, the girls lived with relatives until they graduated from high school, then quickly married and began families of their own. Life went on.

One daughter visited her father once in prison, the other did not. Both exchanged letters with their father, but the communication was mostly superficial and unsatisfactory and eventually tapered off. Both daughters visited their father at the end, just before he died of kidney failure in 1968. The setting was a hospital, and their heavily medicated father was connected to many tubes and a ventilator. If the girls expected a meaningful deathbed conversation, they were sadly disappointed.

Audrey and Pat each describe having a very happy childhood. Their family was normal and they all got along, doing all of the family activities typical of that era. After they moved to Sturgeon Bay, the family lived in houses surrounded by orchards, and the girls recall great times romping with friends and cousins among the fruit trees, even while their mother was hard at work picking apples and cherries for her employer.

Pat has very fond memories of riding with her dad in his gas truck as routine deliveries were made across expansive Door County. Bill's route sometimes required a trip to Washington Island, at the very tip of Door County. There was nothing routine about the exciting, forty-five-minute ferry ride young Patsy took with her dad to reach the island!

If there were problems between their parents, the girls never knew about them. But like a lot of families, then and now, family issues were typically ignored for as long as possible, rather than discussed. Audrey believes that her mother knew fully of her father's affair with Julia Smith, or at least had heard the rumors, but she does not recall any arguments, confrontations, or discussions about it. Probably Margaret Drews chose to hide her pain—to ignore the issue for as long as she could. Problems were swept under the rug.

Throughout her adult years Audrey herself has preferred not to talk about, or even think about, the tragic events that ended her family when she was an adolescent. As a seventeen-year-old, she, along with a maternal aunt, attended her father's trial. Audrey believed in his innocence, until she heard his confession read in court. "I was in shock, didn't care any more." Ever since, she has tried her best to ignore the past. "Let sleeping dogs lie. It's all in the past. What's the point of talking about it? That's the way I've always felt." Whether or not one agrees with her adaptive strategy, Audrey is undoubtedly a survivor. She holds her head high and moves forward.

Pat's approach to life is very different from her sister's, a contrast, I believe, rooted in their differing developmental stages at the time of the double-tragedy in their lives. Audrey was a teenager and surrounded by high school friends, a natural circle of support. But Patsy was just a young child—one day a part of a happy family, a few days later attending her mother's funeral and being sent away to live with relatives. Two years after that, her dad was headed to prison, hated locally and the subject of headlines that scorned him across the nation. The questions that must have swirled in her mind! She was too young to formulate her thoughts into meaningful inquiries, and even if she had asked, no one, on either her mother's or father's side of the family, was willing to answer. Not a single person would even mention her father's name! The unspoken family motto was: Don't even ask, because we're not talking about it.

Not talking, though, predictably led to a lifelong quest for information. Following the death of Sadie Cody, stories replete with gory details appeared nationally in at least a dozen detective magazines, a very popular medium of the day. Anyone in the country who knew how to read could learn everything about the horrific murder at the mansion. But eight-year-old Patsy was left in the dark. For years and years, the magazines and the information they contained were kept from her, *literally*. But one day her curiosity was finally rewarded. Along with her cousin, Patsy found hidden in a closet a detective magazine featuring the Cody murder. They read it secretly, then returned it to the hiding place, careful not to get caught.

Pat actively wonders about the tragic events of her childhood, even though she realizes there will never be any answers for her. She will openly discuss these things—her questions and fears, as well as her frustrations—with any friend, close or casual, who is willing to listen. The tears of her childhood remain.

It is neither logical nor fair to judge parents by the lives of their adult children, or conversely, children by the actions and choices of their parents. Nonetheless, it is impossible to observe the Drews family without recognizing how strongly ingrained the value of "family" is.

Not long after they graduated from high school, both Audrey and Pat married and began families of their own. Collectively, there are ten children and dozens of grandchildren and great-grandchildren, and practically everyone lives within a few miles of each other. When the family gathers for holidays and celebrations, as they frequently do, Margaret is rarely mentioned and Bill's name remains taboo. Yet the two parents are buried side-by-side in the small-town cemetery, and it seems certain that both would be very proud of Audrey and Pat.

Afterword

The old neighborhood is dying! The thought undoubtedly occurred to Harvey Rowe time after time in the decades following Mrs. Cody's murder. In his formative years, young Harvey considered the block of Fifth Avenue between Michigan and Louisiana Streets to be the "center of the universe."

Who could blame Harvey for feeling a loss? He had been the only child of doting parents, one of only a few children on the block and a natural center of attention, if not always delight, for neighbors like the Burkes and McLaughlins. As an adult, he stayed in his childhood home even as neighbors died or moved away, replaced by newcomers who had only a passing notion or interest in the life of Mrs. Cody. The former grandeur of the neighborhood was gone. Eventually Harvey himself, approaching his later years, was forced to move away.

Following the death of Sadie Cody in 1948, her estate went into probate. Appointed as an executor was William E. Wagener, Mrs. Cody's longtime advisor, attorney, and friend. Readers will recall that it was Wagener who tried unsuccessfully during a 1915 discovery hearing to expose Dr. Elmer Robb, Sadie's second husband, as the scoundrel that he was.

In 1949 the Cody mansion was sold to the local chapter of the Veterans of Foreign Wars, and then in 1955 to the Knights of Columbus. Both organizations, but especially the Knights, held meetings in the mansion and even opened up the property for community events such as scout meetings and teen dances. Mrs. Cody liked children and would have been pleased to have the scouts. She distrusted teenagers, however, and would have cringed at the idea of their dancing all over the place! More than once police were called to quell the noise and rowdiness.

153

Rowe and Dodd

Many of today's town residents remember attending events or parties in the mansion and exploring from floor to floor. Surely many curious children ventured into the cellar to investigate the coal-burning furnace and swap tidbits of the gruesome stories they'd heard from their parents and others. An especially pleasant memory of one now-grown resident is of the Knights erecting a freshly painted nativity scene in front of the mansion and hosting a holiday reception.

Over the years, the old house slowly deteriorated, especially the interior with its ornate furnishings. The Knights of Columbus did their best to keep up outside appearances and even painted the entire exterior, quite an undertaking. Fortunately the paint was donated by a local merchant, but unfortunately the color—Belgian blue—was hideous. Grand Knight Gussie Gosser, who lived nearby, explained poetically, "We knew it was a horrible hue, but we got it free so what could we do!"

In 1981 the mansion was sold to John and Dr. Anne B. Jackson. Interior renovations began immediately. Two years earlier, the Jacksons had moved to Sturgeon Bay, where Dr. Jackson set up a medical practice as a specialist. Sadie Cody had always lamented the "lack of medical specialists" in town and blamed it for the death of her husband Richard. Now, not only was the mansion being fixed up but a specialist was moving in! Sadly, things did not work out for the Jacksons, professionally or personally. After owning the mansion less than six months, they sold it and moved out of the area. In its most recent incarnation, the mansion is a popular bed-and-breakfast.

Sadie E. Cody is buried at Bayside Cemetery in Sturgeon Bay, alongside her beloved husband Richard and daughter Irene. There is a large family monument that, fittingly, is the most prominent in the cemetery. Buried not too far from Mrs. Cody are: the Rowe family—Hallie, Anna, and Harvey; Herb Reynolds, the photographer who documented the Cody crime scene and the trial of William Drews; William E. Wagener, Mrs. Cody's trusted advisor and attorney; and her good friend and neighbor, Allie McReynolds.

Furnace Murder

In her will Sadie Cody left the city of Sturgeon Bay $1000, quite a sum of money in those days, to erect a town clock along with a plaque inscribed "CODY MEMORIAL CLOCK. R.P. Cody, S. E. Cody, Irene Cody." Today, more than sixty-five years following her death, the clock still stands. It is suspended from the old town fire station, now a restaurant, adjacent to the old city hall, now the Sturgeon Bay Visitor Center.

Sadie Cody would be delighted to know that the clock she generously donated is still standing, and the plaque bearing her family's name is in good condition, clearly readable by passersby. She might not be so delighted to learn that the clock has not been functional for nearly ten years. The north side of the clock is stuck at 10:32, while the south side ticks off an "hour" every six actual minutes. Like all dysfunctional clocks, Sadie's gift registers the correct time twice per day, or four times if you consider both sides!

I have asked many residents if they know where the "town clock" is. Most answer, "*What* town clock?" Among the few who can answer the question correctly, only the most historically minded associate the clock with the Cody family, despite the small plaque nearby. Only the most historically astute refer to it as the "Cody clock."

In a way, the lack of recognition about the clock is emblematic of how the saga of Sadie Cody and her mansion has faded. Modern-day residents who did not grow up in Sturgeon Bay respond blankly when asked if they know about the Cody mansion or who Mrs. Cody was. The story had never reached a man who rents an apartment in the old Burke home, directly across the street from the mansion. Life-long town residents in their thirties or forties are likely to be unaware, but those in their sixties and seventies can recall stories told by their parents or older siblings. Anyone in his or her eighties, though, actually remembers the grisly murder, the community fear, and the trial of William Drews.

Hallie H. Rowe, Harvey's father, had a storied career even prior to his life in Door County. A veteran of World War I, he survived the 1918 sinking of the Tuscania that claimed the lives of 210 American troops.

155

Rowe and Dodd

After a long career as game warden followed by two terms as sheriff (1945-1948), Hallie was still only fifty-six and hardly ready for retirement. Instead, he ran for Wisconsin State Assembly in 1949 and won, serving from 1950-52. Then he was re-elected as sheriff for two more terms (1951-54) and finally a fifth term (1957-58).

Eventually the sheriff slowed down. For the last ten years of his life, he fought cardiovascular disease, before finally suffering arrest in 1992, at the age of ninety-six.

Anna E. Rowe, Harvey's mother, died in 1986 at age eighty-seven. Like her husband, she endured cardiovascular disease for several years prior to her death.

Readers will recall that Loretta Burke and Alice McLaughlin were neighbors and friends of Sadie Cody's. In the spring of 1948, when they had heard nothing from Mrs. Cody for several days, their concern led them to hound the local police to do something. Finally, Loretta and Alice, along with Sheriff Rowe, discovered Mrs. Cody's incinerated body in the mansion's furnace. Both women testified at the preliminary hearing of William Drews, and Loretta also at the trial.

Loretta Burke died in 1962 of circumstances eerily reminiscent of Sadie's fiery death. March 14 was a characteristically cold day in Sturgeon Bay. Her husband, Lawrence, planned to go ice fishing and was attempting to fill a hand warmer with lighter fluid. Some spilled onto the floor, creating an invisible cloud of fumes. A heavy smoker, Loretta was never far from a lit cigarette, and the room burst into flames. She became a human torch, suffering burns over 80% of her body.

Fortunately, her daughter Doris, who lived upstairs with her own family, was nearby and came to the rescue, wrapping her mother in a blanket and rolling her on the floor. It was also a stroke of luck that the accident occurred shortly after the beginning of the school day—the timing spared Loretta's three grandchildren from having to witness the accident. Unfortunately, Loretta died ten days later at the Milwaukee Burn Center, at the age of seventy.

Furnace Murder

Tragedy wasn't yet over for the Burke family, however. Broken-hearted by the loss of his wife, Lawrence nonetheless returned a few weeks later to his position as chief engineer on a ship in the Great Lakes. Although he had recently received a clean bill-of-health from his physician, he suffered a heart attack shortly thereafter and died on the ship. It was a dreadful year for the Burke grandchildren. Not only did Eddie, Tina, and Tony lose their beloved maternal grandparents, a paternal grandparent died as well.

A minor mystery in the Burke family revolved around the spelling of their name. Lawrence always spelled it "Birk," but Loretta stuck to "Burke." Readers who might be inclined to side with her should consider that she always called herself "Loretta," even though her real first name was "Marettia"!

Two years after Loretta Burke's death, Alice McLaughlin died, albeit less dramatically. She was eighty-two when she succumbed to congestive heart failure in 1964. Her husband Richard died in 1971 at the age of eighty-nine.

~ ~ ~

Harvey Rowe spent his entire adult life trying to live up to the image of his father. It was a tall task. Despite his tumultuous eighth-grade year, Harvey's educational career proceeded nicely. He graduated from Sturgeon Bay High School in 1952 and from the University of Wisconsin-Madison in 1957, with a degree in political science. Later he attended one year of law school at Marquette University in Milwaukee. In 1966, he completed a training program for state budget management at Indiana University-Bloomington.

During the 1960s Harvey served state government as a legislative assistant, and in 1972 became assistant to Harold V. Froehlich, the minority leader of the State Assembly. Later that year Froehlich was elected to the U.S. Congress, but when he lost a re-election bid in 1974, Harvey was out of a job as well. Rowe extended his civic career during the 1970s, serving time as an aide to the state Highway Commission, a consultant to the Department of Public Welfare, a coordinator for an antidrug enforcement program, and a member of the Door County Civil Service Commission. Two things are unclear about his work history in state and local government: how well he was paid and the degree to which his positions amounted to political "patronage."

In the 1980s Harvey returned full-time to Sturgeon Bay to care for his ailing, elderly parents. Out of work, he devoted himself to writing. He had previously written seventeen articles about the workings of state government and published them in the *Door County Advocate*. Now his interests turned to true crime, and he dove headfirst into researching and writing about the most notorious murders in Door County, including the "Cherry Camp Murder" (1948), the Donald Crass murder (1955), and the murders of Grace and Sumner Harris (1953), the latter being the editor of the *Advocate*.

Still, it was the murder of Sadie Cody in 1948, when Harvey was only fourteen, that always held his fascination and eventually became his obsession. Beginning in the early 1990s, he spent a decade writing his manuscript, which was divided into "books"—town history, biography of Sadie Cody, murder mystery, and glowing tribute to Sheriff Rowe. Anyone who knew Harvey during these years was aware of his manuscript, initially titled *About My Father's Business*. Documenting facts became his vocation, and his text steadily grew, expanding at one point to perhaps 500 typewritten pages.

Meanwhile, his beloved mother and father were both suffering from chronic heart conditions, their health in steady decline. Anna went first, and shortly thereafter the father deeded the house at 22 N. Fifth to Harvey. Six years later, Hallie died. Imagine Harvey alone in the house the family had owned since 1942.

Harvey's career in politics in the state capital ended in the early 1970s, but he did not give up easily. Over the next fifteen years he sought office four times, including runs for State Senate (1974), State Assembly (1978), county clerk (1980), and county treasurer (1990). Each time, voters rejected him.

Although he continued to write articles for the local newspaper, he was paid only small amounts, if anything. With little if any income from a pension or social security, he was rapidly running out of funds. In 1995 he was forced to sell the family home and live off the proceeds. By 2001 he was prepared to make a one last play for fame and fortune: His massive manuscript was finally ready for publication. Sadly, though, no publisher was ready for it. In that same year, he ran for mayor of Sturgeon Bay, but he lost once more.

Harvey's financial situation grew bleaker and bleaker, and he was forced to move from one apartment to a cheaper one, finally ending up in subsidized housing. He had trouble paying utility bills and was too proud to ask friends for help, though he accepted reluctantly when they offered. His biggest fear was losing his car and his beloved motorcycle, along with its cherished license plate: "Wis 1." Harvey was big on small numbers, except when they involved his finances.

In the past year, I have interviewed dozens of people who were friends or acquaintances of Harvey's. Everyone has offered an opinion, even though Harvey has been dead for more than ten years. He is described alternatively as: friendly and talkative, reclusive, eccentric, interesting, likable, political, opinionated, animated, comical, and fascinated with law enforcement.

The description that stands out is "alone but not lonely." Everyone who ever met Harvey remembers knowing him, but very few knew him well. Often when I asked someone about Harvey, the response was, "Have you talked to Brad Birmingham?" So I did.

Brad owns Birmingham's Bar, which was clearly Harvey's favorite place. I called and set up a meeting with Brad, hoping to talk to him at the bar for 15-20 minutes. When I arrived the next day, I was shocked to find that Brad had rounded up four people who were more than willing to talk about Harvey. Funny stories and fond memories of their friend were swapped for ninety minutes! It is evident that whenever he was at Birmingham's, Harvey was neither alone nor lonely.

One friend who was particularly close to Harvey offered insightful views of him, especially the effect of his upbringing. As the sheriff's son, Harvey let himself believe that making friends would come easy and that teachers would offer him special concessions. When neither happened, he was puzzled and frustrated. After finishing school, he expected employment opportunities to fall into his lap. Landing his first few political appointments reinforced the notion, but as each job ended he would become indignant, angry, and depressed. He was always trying to prove to his parents that he could be as successful as his father. But Hallie won every election he entered, whereas Harvey failed every time. Having a hero for a dad was both a blessing and a curse.

The last year of his life was a miserable one. He was depressed about his circumstances—unhappy with his living situation, unable to pay bills or buy himself dinner, and frustrated with poor medical care. Dating back to high school, and possibly even to those earlier years when he lived in the jail, Harvey suffered from insomnia, nightmares, and night terrors. Sleeping was rarely restful. In the end, dwelling on his plight caused insomnia, but sleep brought on bizarre and disturbing dreams, such as assassins attempting to murder his fleeing mother. He had little to look forward to during the day, and torment awaited him at day's end.

On January 26, 2004, Harvey Rowe drafted a simple will and had it witnessed by two officials. It consisted of two short paragraphs, sixty words in all. In the morning hours of February 23, Harvey died of a self-inflicted gunshot wound to the head. The gun had once been Sheriff Rowe's service revolver.

# # #

Appendices

Appendix A

Confession of William Drews

After hours of intense questioning by Sheriff Hallie Rowe and others, William Drews confessed to the murder of Sadie Cody on April 6, 1948. There were several witnesses to the confession, including Rowe and District Attorney Ed Minor. During trial, Drews's public defender argued forcefully that the confession had been coerced.

Below is the full three-page confession, as transcribed by District Attorney Ed Minor and signed by William Drews. The statement was given at the Sturgeon Bay City Hall.

My name is William Drews and I live in Sturgeon Bay. On the day aforementioned [April 2] at about 10:30 a.m. in the morning, I came to the door of Mrs. Cody's house and she asked me to come in. I went in to get money from her and went into the big living room. I visited with her, then asked her to lend me some money, when she didn't I hit her with my fist in the face, knocked her out completely on the floor. She bled from the nose and I picked her up, carried her downstairs, opened the furnace door—she was dead when she got in the basement. I came back, was just standing there and the money was in the purse on table.

I put her completely in the furnace but did not monkey in any way with the thermostat.

She went too far away from me when I hit her. I looked in her purse while she was on the floor. I went into the kitchen from the living room. I got $110.00 in purse, it was lying there. I did not go there at first to rob her but just asked her to lend me money because I figured she had money.

Rowe and Dodd

I put her into the furnace headfirst, the furnace was going at the time. I opened the big door—then after, I wiped off my hands in the cistern.

The backdoor was open and the car was on the corner near the church, walked out to the front sidewalk, was in the house about forty-five minutes altogether.

Went up that day to see if I could get some money. If she would have given me some I would not have killed her.

She said she didn't have any money so I struck her, she was standing up, when I hit her she laid on her side, I carried her in my arms, she moaned a little bit—she was dead when she got into basement, no life. Just robbed her purse. Was not drinking at the time and I was strictly sober.

Went downtown to Kellstrom's filling station, then went home, got home about 11:00 and gave wife the money.

Came back up stairs and went out back door. Did not go back.

This statement has been made freely and voluntarily by me on this 6th day of April 1948.

[signed] William Drews

164

Appendix B

Letter from Ed Minor to Parole Board

In 1959 William Drews, seeking release from prison for time served, requested a hearing before the parole board. Edward G. Minor, the district attorney who prosecuted Drews, wrote the following letter in strenuous opposition to Drews's release. At the time he wrote the letter, Ed Minor was a federal prosecutor, officially the U.S. Attorney for the Eastern District of Wisconsin. Copies of Minor's letter were sent to Judge Edward M. Duquaine, who presided at Drews's trial, and Sheriff Hallie Rowe.

May 25, 1959

Division of Corrections
State Department of Public Welfare
Att: Sanger B. Powers, Director
re: Drews, William – WSP #30042

Gentlemen:

I am in receipt of your communication dated May 20, 1959 together with notice of hearing on behalf of the above-named prisoner.

This man was a vicious killer, having put Mrs. Cody in a furnace and burned her while she was still alive. I am also satisfied from the evidence we obtained after his conviction for killing Mrs. Cody that he also murdered his first wife inasmuch as her car was found alongside a road amongst some

165

trees and was burned, the car having been burned only on the side where she had been sitting.

Drews, with the criminal tendencies he has, should never be released, because I am more than certain that if he is released, some other victim will suffer the same fate as the other two. I do not think parole or pardon laws were ever made to fit an individual such as this.

Very truly yours,

Edward G. Minor

Apparently Minor's letter served its purpose. William Drews was denied parole.

Appendix C

Psychiatric Examination of William Drews

On May 12, 1948, twenty days following his entry into state prison, William Drews was examined by a psychiatrist employed by the Division of Corrections. Below are excerpts from the "admission examination." It should be noted that the family history, social history, and history of offense are probably based primarily, if not exclusively, upon Drews's self-report.

Family History. Father was farmer in poor circumstances. 2 brothers and 1 sister.

Social history. First marriage, 1929. Widowed, 1946. Two children. Second marriage, 1948. Wife has four children by previous marriage. School: 8th grade rural school through age 14. Truck driver in poor circumstances. Light drinker.

Military History: None – discharged before training by the Armistice.

History of offense. Pleaded not guilty on lawyer's advice. Had attorney, jury trial, found guilty. "I lost my job with the oil company because they were making crooks out of us and I took about $80 from them. I was going to get married and my sister and a man who owed me money hadn't paid me so I went to see if I could borrow some from this old lady who I knew had plenty. When I asked her for it, she said 'No' and I felt embarrassed and mad because she had so much and

167

wouldn't loan me any so I hit her. Then I got scared and tried to hide the body and couldn't think of any place, so I stuffed it in the furnace."

Prior offenses: This is first arrest and conviction of felony.

Institutional history: Well-adjusted. Reads sports magazines, listens to radio.

Average intelligence (tested 5-7-1948).

Appraisal: This man's personality manifests characteristics of rather suspicious type. . . . Is shallow . . . and emotionally flat. . . . Judgment is totally defective. . . . Complete absence of remorse . . . poor insight. Openly confesses all facts of fatal assault. . . . Denies completely . . . antagonism toward victim. Shows persecutory trends directed primarily toward a former employer with rather lengthy recital of the supposed unethical business practices demonstrated by the group. . . . Has no previous criminal record of any type . . . he evinces no evidence of viciousness. . . .

Acknowledgments

[The first section reflects a partial list of acknowledgments made by Harvey Rowe in the original manuscript. The second section includes acknowledgments by David K. Dodd.]

Acknowledgments by Harvey Rowe

Ann Thorp (deceased) of Fish Creek, Wisconsin, for her advice and counsel in finalizing this manuscript.

Kenneth C. Anderson of Oshkosh, Wisconsin, formerly of Sturgeon Bay, for his research into the early life of Sadie Cody and for his continual encouragement.

Clifford Wills (deceased) of Madison, Wisconsin, who provided some of the picture copies used herein.

Herbert C. Reynolds (deceased) of Sturgeon Bay, who was commissioned by Sheriff Hallie Rowe to photograph the crime scene, and who captured on film the events surrounding the Cody murder.

Craig D. Jones, Nancy J. Emery, and Judy E. Ellenbecker, all former staff at Door County Library, for their assistance while I did research in the Laurie Room.

Sandra Simonar, former Clerk of Courts of Door County, for assistance in obtaining documents relating to Sadie Cody and William Drews.

Rowe and Dodd

Acknowledgments by David K. Dodd

Thanks to all of my great readers: Julie Kudick, Candace Worrick, and John Borrowman III. Julie offered not only the expert view of an author but also the fine eyes of a proofreader. Her advice regarding organization of the book was especially helpful.

Candace was a close friend of Harvey's and knew of his manuscript long before I did. Her insights into Harvey's character and personal history were invaluable, as were her suggestions about the manuscript.

John is a childhood friend who shares my passion for writing. Our days of Little League baseball and garage bands are long past. Now we toss manuscripts back and forth and try to help each other eliminate off-key notes. (A mixed metaphor, I know, John!)

Thank you, Mary Reynolds Aiken, for granting your family's permission to use the many photographs taken by your father, Herbert C. Reynolds. Although Herb was usually behind the camera, he played an important role in the events of April 1948, including documentation of the crime scene at the Cody mansion and the trial of William Drews.

Many people gave generously of their time and knowledge, assisting in various ways. Several were friends of Harvey's who eagerly contributed time, information, and support toward the goal of seeing Harvey's manuscript finally published. These include Roger Anderson, Brad Birmingham, Chuck Brann, John Enigl, Sr., Larry Zessin, and Leo Zipperer. Others who helped in a variety of ways include Tina Hunsader Danielson, Tony Hunsader, Jim Marsh, Arleigh R. Porter, Sally Treichel, and Claudette Weiterman.

A very special thank you to Peggy Dodd, my life companion and constant source of inspiration. She tirelessly read the manuscript in its many versions and always came up with new insights, and corrections!

Audrey and Patsy, thank you for answering my difficult questions graciously and selflessly. You have my complete admiration.

About the Authors

Harvey W. Rowe graduated from the University of Wisconsin-Madison, with a degree in political science. After attending law school at Marquette University in Milwaukee, Wisconsin, he spent several years in state government, serving as a legislative assistant and member on several state commissions and panels. He was also a congressional assistant to U.S. Representative Harold V. Froehlich.

He returned to his hometown of Sturgeon Bay, Wisconsin, during the 1980s and ran for various state and local offices. He was best known locally as a regular contributor to the *Door County Advocate*, especially for his fascinating stories about local murders. Harvey died in 2004.

David K. Dodd, a former psychologist, now writes fiction that focuses on personal conflict, relationships, and community. Following three novels, *Furnace Murder* is his first work of nonfiction. He lives in Fish Creek, Wisconsin.

Other Books by David K. Dodd

Star Shooting. A compelling story of youthful promise, friendship, and family, this novel is a tragicomedy that readers will find both heartbreaking and heartwarming,
[Bay Creek Publishing. ISBN 978-0-9835670-0-4]

Star Dawning. Three separate families, each struggling to survive, connect in ways that are unpredictable and fascinating. An inspiring story of individual redemption and the restorative power of family.
[Bay Creek Publishing. ISBN 978-0-9835670-1-1]

NOY World: A Futuristic Tale of Devastation and Devolution.
Survivors of catastrophic climate change live a dystopian existence dominated by NOY, the ruling class. The human spirit survives, even amid environmental and societal ruin.
[Bay Creek Publishing. ISBN 978-0-9835670-2-8]

CPSIA information can be obtained
at www.ICGtesting.com
Printed in the USA
FSOW03n1406231116
27622FS